The Story So Far

*What We Know About the
Business of Digital Journalism*

Columbia Journalism Review Books

Columbia Journalism Review Books
Series Editors Evan Cornog and Victor Navasky

Columbia
Journalism
School ♔

Tow Center
for
Digital
Journalism

The Story So Far

What We Know About the
Business of Digital Journalism

A REPORT BY

Bill Grueskin
Dean of Academic Affairs, Columbia Journalism School

Ava Seave
Principal, Quantum Media
Adjunct Associate Professor, Columbia Business School

Lucas Graves
Ph.D. Candidate, Columbia Journalism School

Columbia University Press New York

Columbia University Press
Publishers Since 1893
New York   Chichester, West Sussex
cup.columbia.edu

Library of Congress Cataloging-in-Publication Data
A complete Cataloging-in-Publication record is available from the Library of Congress

ISBN 978-0-231-16027-8 (pbk.: alk. paper)
ISBN 978-0-231-50054-8 (e-book)

∞
Columbia University Press books are printed on permanent and durable acid-free paper.
Printed in the United States of America

Table of Contents

Introduction

Few news organizations can match the setting of the Miami Herald. The paper's headquarters is perched on the edge of Biscayne Bay, offering sweeping views of the islands that buffer the city of Miami from the Atlantic Ocean. Pelicans and gulls float near the building; colorful cruise ships ply the waters a few miles away.

And Miami Herald executives long held some of the best views in the city, from the fifth floor of the company's headquarters.

Not any longer.

The Herald, like most U.S. daily newspapers, has faced severe financial troubles in recent years, suffering deep cuts in the newsroom and other departments. So, in one of many efforts to raise revenue, executives attached a billboard to the east side of the Herald building, completely obscuring the bay views of many newspaper employees, including the publisher.

The benefits of the billboard are obvious: the low six figures in annual revenue, according to a Herald executive, or enough to pay the salaries of a few junior reporters.

The irony is obvious as well, for the advertiser buying the space is Apple—the company that now controls a commerce and publishing system crucial to the future of the news business. And the product being advertised on the Herald's wall is the iPad, a device that is both disruptive and helpful to media economics.

Indeed, the two companies provide a way to see the destruction and creation in the media business over the past decade. At the end of March 2001, the stock market valued the Herald's parent company, Knight-Ridder, at almost precisely the same amount as Apple: $3.8 billion.

Ten years later, Apple's valuation is more than $300 billion. And Knight-Ridder no longer exists as an independent company.[1]

Miami Herald building, with Herald logo on right and Apple iPad billboard on left, April 2011   (*Jeff Binion photo*)

* * *

The difficult financial state of the U.S. news industry is no longer new. Most big newsrooms have faced severe cutbacks, and even though online-only outlets have sprung up in communities throughout the country, they haven't fully taken the place of what has been lost.

These issues were explored in a precursor report[2] to this one, sponsored by Columbia University's Graduate School of Journalism and written by Leonard Downie Jr., former executive editor of the Washington Post, and Michael Schudson, a professor at Columbia. At the end of that report, which was published in late 2009, the authors provided a number of recommendations to stanch the losses in independent reporting.

Most of the recommendations were based in policy, including changes in the tax code to provide news organizations easier access to nonprofit status and encouraging philanthropists to support news gathering. Most controversially,

Downie and Schudson recommended the creation of a national "Fund for Local News" supported with fees the Federal Communications Commission would collect from telecom users, broadcast licensees or Internet service providers.

That suggestion drew praise from some, as well as criticism from those who saw it as an intrusion by the government in a free and robust press. In the words of Seth Lipsky,[3] editor of the New York Sun, "The best strategy to strengthen the press would be to maximize protection of the right to private property—and the right to competition. Subsidies are the enemy of competition."

This report stands on the shoulders of the first one, but takes a different approach. Without addressing the merits of philanthropists or governments supporting news gathering,[4] we wanted to address another question: What kinds of digitally based journalism in the U.S. is the commercial market likely to support, and how?

While this report will examine some traditional, or "legacy," business models for media, our focus is on the economic issues that news organizations—large and small, old and new—face with their digital ventures.

This report focuses on news organizations that do original journalism, defined for our purposes as independent fact-finding undertaken for the benefit of communities of citizens. Those communities can be defined in the traditional way, by geography, but can also be brought together by topics or commonalities of interest. We also look into media companies that aggregate content and generate traffic in the process.

We confine our report mostly to for-profit news enterprises. We recognize the outstanding work done by such national organizations as ProPublica and the Center for Investigative Reporting, as well as local sites like Voice of San Diego and MinnPost. But for the purposes of this study, we felt it was more valuable to spend our time examining organizations that rely as much as possible on the commercial market.

We do have a bias: We think the world needs journalism and journalists. We welcome the tremendous access people now have to data and information, but much of what Americans need to know will go unreported and unexposed without skilled, independent journalists doing their work. That work can include reporting and editing in the traditional way, as well as aggregating information from other sources, or sorting and presenting data to make it accessible and understandable.

We decided to restrict our studies mostly to the U.S. market. We found the domestic news scene to be a rich and textured one, with plenty of complexity of its own, though we appreciate that a great deal of innovation is taking place beyond U.S. borders.

We define digital journalism broadly. While many publishers still see it as an online phenomenon—that is, displaying content on a PC screen via the Internet—we have included other platforms, including mobile phones and tablets.

We found several challenges in preparing this study. First, while a great deal of data about digital ventures is available, much of it is unverifiable. Small startups and other private companies have no legal reporting requirements, so some of the figures we cite here are taken with appreciation and on good faith. Further, digital revenue is still such a small sliver of the total for publicly traded companies that, when it is broken out at all, it is rarely displayed in such a way that reveals how much comes from a particular station or publication. And, it often isn't clear how much of a company's stated digital revenue represents genuinely new income as opposed to legacy dollars reapportioned to online businesses.

We sought to make this report accessible to newcomers and useful to those who have spent years in this field. We have tried to explain such terms as "CPM" (cost per thousand of views) and "impressions" (advertising spaces that appear on a digital page) in the text. And we have tried to be as rigorous as possible in examining numbers that media companies provide when describing their digital results. We also consulted a number of secondary sources to provide background and data unavailable elsewhere. These included important texts from the dawn of the digital age, such as Stewart Brand's "The Media Lab,"[5] and more recent books, such as James Hamilton's "All The News that's Fit to Sell"[6] and "Information Rules"[7] by Carl Shapiro and Hal R. Varian. Of course, we also relied on more current sources, particularly such sites as paidcontent.org, niemanlab.org and cjr.org.

But the bulk of the research in this report is based on a series of interviews we did in late 2010 and early 2011. We visited mainstream print and broadcast organizations with rich histories and Pulitzers and duPonts lining the walls; we also interviewed the founders and editors of innovative new journalistic enterprises. In most cases, publishers and editors were open, candid and willing to be quoted on the record. In a few instances, we decided to trade confidentiality for access to internal numbers or insights that would not otherwise be available.

We recognize, finally, that digital journalism is such a dynamic field that some of the findings and conclusions we reach in May 2011 will be outdated within months. That is what makes this subject so fertile for researchers and so humbling for seers. And we conclude our study not with predictions but with recommendations for how news businesses large and small, new and old, can more effectively meet the challenges brought on by the digital transformation.

---

[1] Apple's split-adjusted stock price was about $10 (from Yahoo Finance, http://yhoo.it/ecaGAO), while Knight-Ridder's was around $60 (Grain Market Research, http://bit.ly/dGf5F5). Apple had far more shares outstanding, leading to valuations that are within 1 percent of each other.

[2] Entire contents of "The Reconstruction of American Journalism" can be found on CJR.org, http://bit.ly/eP6Fjl

[3] "All the News That's Fit to Subsidize," op-ed from WSJ.com, Oct. 21, 2009. http://online.wsj.com/article/SB10001424052748704597704574486242417039358.html

[4] Media commentator Alan Mutter addressed this in a post, "Non-profits can't possibly save the news," Reflections of a Newsosaur, March 30, 2010, http://bit.ly/dMp86C. He calculated the news media would need an endowment of $88 billion to produce enough revenue to support current models.

[5] Stewart Brand, The Media Lab (Penguin, 1988).

[6] James Hamilton, All the News that's Fit to Sell (Princeton University Press, 2003).

[7] Carl Shapiro and Hal R. Varian, Information Rules (Harvard Business School Press, 1999).

Chapter One

News from Everywhere: *The Economics of Digital Journalism*

In early 2005, a researcher at the Poynter Institute published a column that was instantaneously read and—by many—misunderstood.[1]

Rick Edmonds, who studies the financial side of the news business for Poynter's website, speculated about how long it would take for online newspaper revenue to match the dollars brought in by the print side. He estimated that digital ads accounted for around 3 percent of the total revenue for an average U.S. paper. Edmonds assumed an optimistic online growth rate, around 33 percent a year, and what seemed then to be a reasonably sober estimate of print growth, around 4 percent.

High hopes

In 2005, an analyst projected how long it might take for a typical newspaper's online revenue to match its print revenue.
Even assuming optimistic annual growth of 33.3% online and 4% print, it would take 14 years.

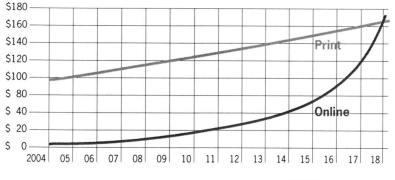

SOURCE: Poynter.org analysis

Given how low online sales were at the time, Edmonds noted it would take 14 years for digital revenue to catch up to that of print. As he wrote, these calculations provided "little cause for cheer." He also noted "there isn't any reason to believe any of these numbers will remain steady state over time."

His disclaimers were lost on many readers. At several conferences later that year, participants pointed to the study and cheered one of the presumptions in the column—that digital revenue would grow by a third every year, as far as the eye could see.

For a few years, it seemed as if this scenario might be realistic. Newspapers' online revenue grew by more than 30 percent in both 2005 and 2006.[2] But growth slowed the next year, came to a halt during the recession and still hasn't fully returned to what it was in 2007. Meanwhile, print revenue hasn't grown at 4 percent a year since 2005; indeed, newspapers' print revenue in 2010 was less than half what it was in 2005.

Fifteen years after most news organizations went online, it is clear that old media business models have been irrevocably disrupted and that the new models are fundamentally different from what they once were. What made traditional media so vulnerable to the Web? Or perhaps the better question is this: Why has digital technology, which has been such a powerful force for transmitting news, not yet provided the same energy for companies to maintain and increase profits?

Mainstream news organizations had already started losing audience before the Internet became popular. Broadcast network news programs have been sliding steadily since 1980 and now reach slightly over 20 million viewers a night, down more than half in three decades. Newspapers began to experience significant circulation declines decades ago. Total daily newspaper circulation has fallen by 30 percent in 20 years, from 62.3 million in 1990 to 43.4 million in 2010, as people found other sources, particularly local television news, to be an adequate substitute.[3]

Revenue, however, held steady or increased for mainstream news outlets, even as audiences shrank. This was true in the early days of the Web, too, thanks in part to an advertising bubble spawned by the Internet boom.

To begin to understand the disruptions of the digital transformation, it is important to appreciate the circumstances that made the news business—whether in broadcast, cable, magazines or newspapers—so profitable for so long. The commercial heyday that buoyed the fortunes of American newsrooms in the last half-century had its roots in changes that began much earlier.

Through the 19th Century, newspapers benefited from economic and demographic shifts that accompanied industrialization—in particular, rapid urbanization and the attendant rise of the big-city retail economy. The growing advertising market encouraged urban publishers, who had begun to loosen their ties to political parties and to think of themselves as independent businesspeople. In the process, they realized they could make most of their money from local retailers, rather than from people in the street paying a few pennies to buy their papers.

Historians of journalism argue that these economic and political shifts underpinned an increasingly professionalized and objective journalism that became the norm in the 1920s and 1930s. The move toward general-interest, advertising-supported newspapers aimed at broad audiences also drove a cycle of concentration and consolidation that would continue for decades.

With audiences and ad revenue growing even as competitors disappeared, newsrooms and newspapers swelled in size. An analysis of major metropolitan dailies by the American Journalism Review found that between 1965 and 1999, eight of the 10 newspapers studied saw at least one competitor disappear.[4] During the same period, on average, each of the surviving newspapers doubled the amount of news it produced. Even as new or expanded sections—sports, business, lifestyle—claimed a larger share of each edition, the total coverage of local, national and international news continued to increase.

The trend of increasing consolidation in a growing advertising market helped to compensate for declining readership. By the early 1980s, most U.S. cities had just one daily newspaper. Or, in markets with two papers, one was clearly dominant and the other was kept afloat by favorable terms negotiated in joint operating agreements that Congress had created to preserve local journalistic competition. Radio and television newsrooms enjoyed similar access to a lucrative market. The advertising business in broadcast was so strong that even television and radio stations with small market shares were profitable; those with a strong command of the audience were cash machines.

The monopoly or oligopoly that most metropolitan news organizations enjoyed by the last quarter of the 20th Century meant they could charge high rates to advertisers, even if their audiences had shrunk. If a local business needed to reach a community to promote a sale or announce a new store, the newspaper and TV station were usually the best way to do it. Even if the station or newspaper could deliver only 30 percent of the local market, down from 50 percent a decade earlier, that was still a greater share than any other single medium could provide.

That changed after 2001. The recession that followed the September 11 attacks forced many companies to cut spending, reducing media companies' advertising stream. More importantly, the digital transformation accelerated, and more users began to get their news, for free, on personal computers. The link between a consumer's getting the news and a provider's expensive investment in publishing, broadcast and delivery was broken; this brought a flood of new competitors. Craigslist helped devastate classified ads, newspapers' most lucrative source of revenue, and in 2008, the deep recession fueled by the financial crisis undermined real estate and employment advertising.

As we get further into the digital age, we can more plainly see how the transformation has affected news organizations and the citizens who depend on them. Consumers certainly have benefited—they have more choices, speedier delivery of news and more platforms. But as legacy companies shrink, these advantages have often been accompanied by a loss of original news coverage. New entrants have achieved impressive editorial results, but not many of them have achieved financial stability without some philanthropic or other non-market support.

The move to digital delivery has transformed not just the business of news, but also the way news is reported, aggregated, distributed and shared. Each of those changes has an underlying economic rationale, and the media industry has sometimes been slow to recognize the changes or has been paralyzed by their impact.

Below, we list some of the most consequential changes brought on by the digital era and offer thoughts on how they will affect the way journalism is supported in the years to come.

I. A Different Business

- **Digital requires a new way of thinking about your audience, one that now feasts on an abundance of information.** In the words of Syracuse University Professor Vin Crosbie, "Within the span of a single human generation, people's access to information has shifted from relative scarcity to surplus."[5] As Crosbie notes, it isn't enough simply to transfer content from a legacy platform to a new one. Digital journalism requires an entirely different mind-set, one that recognizes the plethora of new options available to consumers. Tom Woerner, a senior vice president at freelance-generated site Examiner.com, notes that "the old distribution model allowed for only so much content. There are only so many pages you can print, only so many minutes you can sell in a broadcast. ... Now the limits are gone, for both good and bad."

  Impact: Readers have access to far more information than they used to, almost always for free. But for publishers, the competition is nearly infinite, meaning much of the news has become a commodity, with pricing to match.

- **Digital is where the users are heading.** In the most recent study by the Pew Research Center for the People & the Press, 65 percent of people ages 18 to 29 get their news from the Internet—outpacing television for the first time and far exceeding the 21 percent in that age group who rely primarily on newspapers.[6] Among people ages 50 to 64, the Internet (34 percent) and newspapers (38 percent) are almost tied. The Web's growing popularity means the "network effect" can kick in. That is, as more people use news sites, those sites become more valuable to their users, especially as readers and viewers comment on—and contribute to—stories. Meanwhile, more usage is gravitating from computer screens to smartphones, tablets and other mobile devices. According to a January 2011 Pew study, 47 percent of American adults say they get at least some local news and information on their cellphone or tablet computer.[7]

Impact: Digital platforms provide ways for audiences to build quickly with lower marketing costs than in traditional media. And the shift to mobile provides news organizations with more opportunities for targeted content and advertising. But increased audiences don't always lead to proportional gains; in other words, more people may be viewing a site, but that doesn't mean revenue increases to the same or greater degree. Witness a recent report by McClatchy Co., the third-largest newspaper firm in the U.S. The company said the number of local daily unique visitors to its websites grew by 17.3 percent in 2010, yet digital revenue rose only 2.4 percent for the year.[8] And mobile ad sales have so far been less lucrative than those on Internet platforms. Chris Hendricks, vice president of interactive media for McClatchy, says that "seven percent of our traffic comes from mobile. The traffic is significant, the revenue is not."

- **Digital provides a means to innovate rapidly, determine audience size quickly and wind down unsuccessful businesses with minimal expense.** The substantial capital expenditures that used to be involved in starting a new media company are largely gone. A video service need not build tall antennae atop the highest hills in town, and print publishers can avoid capital-intensive investments in printing presses. The large staffs associated with getting information to readers—whether they're camera crews or printing staffs—aren't as necessary. It took Sports Illustrated at least 10 years to get its formula right and become profitable[9]; it took Huffington Post less than six years to go from an idea to a valuation of $315 million in its 2011 sale to AOL.

  Impact: The development time from idea to market is shortened, greatly increasing efficient use of a firm's resources. But because competitors can imitate or adapt more quickly, it is difficult to cash in on innovations. The shorter cycles can lessen the length of time that innovations remain unique, relevant and valuable.

- **Digital platforms extend the lifespan of journalism.** In the analog era, news stories were as ephemeral as fruit flies. An article was prominent for a day, then available only on a library's microfiche; a video would be broadcast to millions on the nightly news, then it would be sent to a network's vault. Journalism now can be freely accessible for as long as a publisher wills it to be. In the words of one programmer, "There is no such thing as 'yesterday's news.'"

Impact: News organizations can make money from their archives as part of a subscription or pay-per-view service, or as part of a scheme to provide more content and build traffic and ad revenue. But as increasing amounts of content stream into archives, consumers may have greater difficulty finding what they want.

II. Content and Distribution: A Fundamental Change

- **Digital disrupts the aggregation model that was so profitable for so long.** Almost no one used to read the entire newspaper every morning, and audiences frequently tuned in and out of the network news at night. Yet, news organizations sold their advertising as if every page was turned and every moment was viewed. Indeed, print publications applied a multiplier—often up to 2.5 readers—to account for the audience for each edition they sold. But in the online world, content has become atomized, with each article existing independently of the next. It is as seamless for a reader to go from a tallahasseedemocrat.com story to a video on msnbc.com as it is to read back-to-back stories in Esquire magazine. The economic consequences of this fickle information-gathering are devastating for legacy news organizations, especially because they have ceded many of the benefits of aggregation to sources like Drudge Report, Huffington Post and Google News. Says Michael Golden, vice chairman and president of the New York Times Co.: "We've lost the power of the package."[10]

  Impact: News relevant to a particular audience can be assembled cheaply and easily, with significant benefit for readers seeking divergent and even competing points of view. But low-cost aggregators compete with content creators for page views, and often win. In the words of Aaron Kushner, an investor trying to buy the Boston Globe, "The definition of a competitor now is someone who gives away your story for free."

- **Journalists today can find readers wherever there is access to the Internet.** This is an enormous transformation after a century in which the reach of print journalism was limited by a company's printing plants and trucks, and most broadcast news was tied to narrow geographic areas. Even when local newspapers expanded their circulation far beyond their metropolitan areas, the results were usually disappointing—the more geographically distant the reader, the less loyalty and interest in the content. (Three national newspapers—USA Today, the New York Times and the Wall Street Journal—avoided most of those constraints by delivering national rather than local news in authoritative, attractive packages.) By contrast, publishing online means that any article or video will become immediately available around the world, at no added cost. Meanwhile, broadcast outlets' reach, once defined largely by geographic and bandwidth constraints and enforced by regulatory agencies, is expanding. Their content is no longer limited to local markets and thus is less restricted by federal regulations.

Impact: Journalists and media companies can go where the audience is, expanding markets at low costs. But the advantages that went along with distribution limits—such as protection against new competitors—are disappearing.

- **Digital platforms enable publishers to deploy their readers and viewers in publicizing and distributing their content.** Print publishers used to tout the "pass-along audience"—people who didn't buy a magazine or newspaper but picked it up in, say, a dentist's office, and could therefore be counted as readers. Advertisers were often skeptical of the numbers, which depended on surveys of readers trying to remember if they read a publication they didn't pay for. But digital news organizations can track precisely how people share content—a few years ago mainly by email, and now also by social media like Facebook and Twitter. For journalists, such distribution helps validate and publicize their work.

Impact: Publishers get free distribution with excellent, real-time information. At the same time, they are losing control of the distribution platform that generated such healthy profits. And they have less say over how their content is portrayed; sometimes users post links and add a dollop of nasty criticism.

III. What's Happening To Consumers?

- **News organizations can more easily build new audiences centered on specialized topics or interests.** Because everything online is instantaneously and ubiquitously available, it's far easier to create offerings of more focused content and find users no matter where they live. Fans of a city's football team may be spread around the world, but a news organization can build a site that will draw a substantial audience.

Impact: Highly focused audiences can provide more value to advertisers. But separating audiences into too many niches can bring on a new set of problems. Consumers may find that dealing with multiple content providers—with few guideposts to judge the quality or authority of the source—isn't worth the bother.

- **Publishers have more information about their readers, in real time.** Whether a citizen is using free Google Analytics on a blog, or a mainstream organization is deploying more sophisticated usage-tracking services like Omniture or Chartbeat, journalists know much more about who's viewing their content, where the audience is coming from and how it is engaged. Unfortunately, many of these numbers are unreliable, misconstrued and prone to exaggeration. Usage estimates often vary by 200 percent or more. This issue was explored in detail in a report last year by Columbia University's Tow Center for Digital Journalism.[11] Metrics have always been challenging for advertisers, especially in the broadcast world. But as the Tow report notes, digital media have failed to come up with common standards; they have not yet settled on metrics, whatever their flaws, as broadcast media did generations ago. "It is a long-appreciated irony of media measurement that accuracy matters less than consensus," the report said. "Doubts don't matter much as long as no competitor is seen to benefit."

Impact: Media companies can measure the popularity of articles, videos or sections and adjust their strategy to maximize revenue and audience. But uncertainty around metrics inhibits advertisers from investing fully in the digital marketplace and depresses advertising rates for those who do take part.

- **Digital platforms fundamentally change the customer experience, in ways that are both advantageous and harmful for news organizations' economics.** Publishers can now capture highly valuable bits of user information, ranging from areas of interest to credit-card numbers. But new media rarely provide the immersive experience found in traditional platforms. Many users keep numerous sites open on tabs in their Internet browsers and don't focus on any one for very long; they often come to a news site through a search and quickly leave for another. Links to other sites provide value to readers but also send them elsewhere, sometimes never to return.

  Impact: By tailoring content and advertising, publishers can charge higher rates to advertisers and win greater loyalty from users. But privacy concerns may lead to regulations that will limit the information publishers can glean about their users. And most readers spend far less time on digital sites than they did on legacy platforms, so news organizations have less opportunity to attract advertising dollars. In the words of Steve Harbula, an editor at Examiner.com: "Readers have a large appetite but a short attention span."

IV. Cutting Costs And Seeking Revenue

- **Digital upsets media's typical pattern of high fixed costs and low variable costs.** It costs a lot—and often requires companies to take on a great deal of debt—to produce the first copy of a newspaper or magazine. But the second copy, and the thousands or millions that follow, are relatively cheap. In the digital realm, many of those initial costs are eliminated, and in some instances—such as starting a blog—they decline to zero.

  Impact: This is a particular challenge for companies that have sunk mounds of cash or taken on debt to make acquisitions that have high fixed costs; those publishers now find such investments to be drags on profitability. Their digital competitors aren't saddled with the same disadvantages.

- **Digital enables news organizations to trim the cost of doing journalism,** particularly if they can get citizens to provide content by bringing them into news production or encouraging them to participate on comment boards.

Impact: Since news and content supplied by paid professionals begets free content by readers/users, the average cost to produce a page view is driven lower. But the quality, accuracy and authority of this content are highly variable and susceptible to manipulation.

- **On digital platforms, it is often hard to make sure that advertising supply matches demand.** Online editors frequently have a difficult time generating enough page views when advertisers demand them—or filling up that advertising space when reader traffic soars and ad demand is light. So news sites often need to run cheap ads, called "remnants," that may get a tenth of the revenue their usual ads draw. Michael Barrett, the CEO of Admeld, a company that tries to increase advertising rates on sites with traffic prone to peaks and valleys, says that some of his clients view the situation "like seats on an airplane. They don't want to fly the plane with any empty seats."

Impact: Because the cost of creating each additional page is close to zero, media companies can have a wide range of prices, charging the highest rates for the most desirable times, placement and audience. But all those unpredictable page views exert constant downward pressure on ad prices.

- **Advertising is transformed in a digital format, and not always for the better.** Some journalists may not realize this, but many of their readers and viewers see advertising as useful and entertaining. Indeed, access to advertising is another incentive for people to buy magazines and newspapers or listen to and watch broadcasts. But the appeal of online advertising is often diminished by its format. A small, rectangular banner ad conveys little useful information—certainly less than an insert in a newspaper or a glossy ad in a fashion magazine. To get useful information from an online ad, a reader often must click and head to a new site, something people rarely do. And the more intrusive forms of online advertising—such as "roadblock" messages that take over the entire screen for a few seconds—upset the user experience. Some digital companies are bringing content value to ads, but they tend not to be news media. Google became a powerhouse by tying advertising directly to users' search queries. And Groupon, which attracts readers who are looking for online discount coupons, has become successful with witty come-ons and obvious value. Groupon has expanded rapidly into hundreds of markets and has turned down a $6 billion offer from Google.[12]

Impact: Digital provides the ability to target advertisers' messages and better metrics to determine impact. But users find that many digital ads on news sites convey little information and value.

- **Digital platforms provide another way for advertising departments to attract new clients and retain old ones.** For salespeople who don't feel they have enough arrows in their quiver, online and mobile can be a way to get a reluctant advertiser into the fold.

Impact: Media companies can bolster more profitable legacy sales in traditional media by adding digital, and in the process, can move their clients to newer platforms. But deals that combine legacy and digital ad sales make it difficult to determine how much revenue is truly attributable to new media. At some companies, half of digital sales have been "bundled" with print or broadcast, and the way those dollars are apportioned can be largely at the whim of the accountants, rather than being an accurate reflection of the value of the ads.

- **Many efforts to get readers to pay for content have been fitful, poorly executed and motivated more by ideology than economics.** Only a few publications have had a successful, long-term plan to get readers to pay, and even fewer have done it in a way that genuinely increases online revenue rather than simply protects their traditional businesses. Was free content journalism's "original sin"?[13] Perhaps, for news organizations must now ask readers to start paying for material that has been free for 15 years. Meanwhile, pay-per-article schemes, such as the one proposed in a 2009 Time cover story by Walter Isaacson, haven't caught on for journalism.[14] Unlike Beatles songs, news stories have little lasting value beyond a single use.

Impact: Users have unlimited access to most content, and publishers have unlimited access to most users. But circulation revenue, one of the mainstays of the traditional media business, has withered. And one of the methods that advertisers have used to judge audience quality—willingness to pay—has evaporated as well.

* * *

As one looks at this list, it becomes clear that most of the economic disadvantages have been fully realized at news organizations, while many of the benefits—such as a surge in mobile-phone advertising—are more potential than real. At the same time, some new models are emerging that can replace some, if not all, of the revenue news organizations have relied upon. Journalists and publishers, new and old, are responding to this new environment in a variety of ways. We'll examine how they have coped, transformed and endeavored to meet the challenges of the digital era.

---

[1] Rick Edmonds, "An Online Rescue for Newspapers?", Poynter.org, Jan. 27, 2005. http://bit.ly/gphsCR

[2] Figures from Newspaper Association of America data. http://bit.ly/h4dxxf

[3] "State of the News Media 2011: Network by the Numbers," Pew Research Center's Project for Excellence in Journalism. http://bit.ly/eH71Ld

[4] Carl Sessions Stepp, "State of the American Newspaper, Then and Now," American Journalism Review, September 1999. http://bit.ly/eDev0Y

[5] Vin Crosbie, "The Placebo Called Convergence," June 9, 2010. http://bit.ly/ft8f8b

[6] "Internet Gains on Television as Public's Main News Source," Pew Research Center for the People & the Press, Jan. 4, 2011. http://bit.ly/ia45aw

[7] "State of the News Media 2011: Mobile News and Paying Online," Pew Research Center's Project for Excellence in Journalism. http://bit.ly/fsVAWf

[8] "McClatchy Reports Fourth Quarter 2010 Earnings," Feb. 8, 2011. http://bit.ly/hsfERQ

[9] Edwin Diamond, "Trouble in Paradise," New York Magazine, March 3, 1986, page 52. http://bit.ly/hPZgZP

[10] Remarks made at Borrell Associates Local Online Advertising Conference, March 3, 2011.

[11] Lucas Graves et al, "Confusion Online: Faulty Metrics and the Future of Digital Journalism," September 2010. http://bit.ly/hBPwt7

[12] A study of local online media has this to say: "Content is king, but not the content most people think. News and information sites do indeed generate revenue, but the top five local online companies derive all their content from their own advertisers." From "Benchmarking Local Online Media: 2010 Revenue Survey," Borrell Associates.

[13] Alan D. Mutter, "Mission Possible? Charging for Web Content," Reflections of a Newsosaur, Feb. 8, 2009. http://bit.ly/gMqNxP

[14] Walter Isaacson, "How to Save Your Newspaper," Time, Feb. 5, 2009. http://ti.me/etDZzr

Chapter 2

The Trouble with Traffic: *Why Big Audiences Aren't Always Profitable*

At first glance, the numbers don't seem to add up: The New York Times has more than 30 million online readers and weekday circulation of less than 900,000 newspapers. Yet, the print edition still accounts for more than 80 percent of the Times' revenue.[1] A broader recent study revealed the same phenomenon: It showed that the Internet occupied 28 percent of Americans' time spent in media in 2009 but generated only 13 percent of total advertising spending.[2]

To understand why, it's important to realize that the prices advertisers pay digital news organizations depend on many factors. Some are tied to the overall market, especially the vast and growing amount of ad space (or inventory) that's available online. Other factors have to do with a site's own dynamics, including the size of the audience it reaches and that nature of that audience—its demographics, how much time its users spend with the site and so on.

So, the Web offers a lot of advantages to publishers and advertisers. But its audiences are more wide than deep.

Journalists constantly feel the push and pull of these numbers. "What am I today?" asks Jeff Cohen, editor of the Houston Chronicle. "I'm an aggregator of eyeballs. ... We're doing around 79 million page views a month—almost a billion in a year." Yet, for all that Web traffic, his newsroom's 206 employees are about half the number employed in 2006.

Digital numbers are confusing when compared with traditional media metrics and are often inflated for all sorts of reasons. Users can be counted several times if they deploy multiple devices, such as a PC, laptop and mobile phone, to access a site. Also, many people delete their computers' "cookies," small text files that allow them to be identified and tracked; because of that, they appear to be new visitors to sites rather than returning ones.[3]

For all that, digital audiences usually far outnumber those from a traditional outlet. As a result, the industry faces a perplexing set of questions: Why do so many digital users generate so little advertising revenue? Is it simply that digital systems are more efficient than the previous oligopolies of the print and broadcast world? Or is there something more fundamentally askew about the way media companies make money off digital customers? And, more importantly, what should publishers be doing to make the most of the readers and viewers they have?

*   *   *

At its most basic level, advertising is a numbers game. A news organization needs a certain number of readers or viewers, and the more it gets, the more ads it can sell and the more it can charge those advertisers. Users also spend varying amounts of time with the magazine, newspaper or broadcast, and the more time they spend, the more an advertiser values the audience.

Digital platforms, thanks to their ubiquity and ease of use, are terrific at the first part of the numbers game. News sites have demonstrated the ability to attract huge numbers of users. And in the first decade of the digital era, particularly as search engines became more powerful, publishers and broadcasters focused on building a mass audience. They poured resources into search engine optimization—the term used to describe a way to improve the odds that headlines will be picked up by Google or other search sites and that topics will be timely enough to appear prominently on a results page. News sites initially welcomed aggregators, such as Drudge Report and Huffington Post, that linked to their material and increased traffic.

As a consequence, audience sizes swelled, and publishers have proclaimed that to be a success. So when the Los Angeles Times in March 2011 logged a record 195 million page views, clicked on by 33 million users, the site's managing editor took a moment to proudly announce those statistics on the site.[4]

But within such numbers is another, less happy, story. The arithmetic shows that each latimes.com user clicked on an average of six pages in March—or just one page every fifth day of the month. That statistic demonstrates how the other essential part of the advertising business—the amount of time and attention that users pay to a site—has been undermined by some of the tactics that publishers have used to attract large audiences.

The phenomenon is widespread. A 2010 Pew analysis of Nielsen media statistics depicts depressingly low levels of usage, even at outstanding national sites. "The average visitor spends only 3 minutes, 4 seconds per session on the typical news sites," the study says.[5] "No one keeps visitors very long." And at top-trafficked news sites, ranging from Yahoo News to the Washington Post to Fox News, most people visit just a few times per month. Compare that to the media of past decades. A 2005 study showed that about half of U.S. newspaper readers spent more than 30 minutes reading their daily paper. And most of the less-devoted readers spent at least 15 minutes with the paper.[6]

There are many reasons for the problems news sites have in getting reader attention, also known as engagement. Consumers today have many digital options available. The experience of getting news on a computer or mobile device, thus far, is fundamentally different from the experience in TV or print; most users tend to flit from site to site, rarely alighting for more than a brief spell.

But there's another way to look at these numbers, one that is more complex—and, in some ways, more encouraging—for the journalism business.

One person studying this issue closely is Matt Shanahan, an analyst who is relatively new to the media world. Shanahan is, by training, an electrical engineer, and he spent much of his career consulting for big businesses in the fields of aerospace and finance. In 2008, he joined a Seattle-area firm called Scout Analytics; the company was looking to serve industries that were failing to realize their potential in the digital world. "The e-commerce market was noisy and crowded," he says. "Media and information, however, were mature industries facing severe revenue issues." Scout figured it could find new clients among media companies that were trying to learn more about the real nature of their digital audiences. The company signed up about 70 news and information sites—some geared to consumers, but more of them in the business-to-business category—and started looking at the activity of users. They were able to track consumers' paths through sites and to figure out how often they visited and what they did on each visit. Shanahan was soon struck by an anomaly of the online news industry: the yawning maw that separates the size of audiences from the level of engagement those readers and viewers demonstrate.

Shanahan points to a website for a 90,000-circulation newspaper that serves a medium-sized city on the East Coast. (The name of the company is confidential because it's a client.) This site gets around 450,000 unique visitors a month.[7] But those visitors differ widely, and Shanahan separates them into four types: The most loyal are the "fans," who visit at least twice a week. Then there are the "regulars," good for one or two visits a week. Sliding down the loyalty scale are "occasionals," who stop by two or three times a month; and finally, the "fly-bys," who come about once a month.

The most loyal visitors are a very small part of the overall audience: Fans make up about 4 percent of the total number of visitors, and regulars 3 percent. Occasionals account for 17 percent and fly-bys for more than 75 percent of the total. In other words, more than three-fourths of the people who visit this news site do so about once a month.

Then Shanahan went deeper, to see how the different kinds of users behaved on the site. He knew the most loyal fans would generate more page views than the fly-bys, since fans visit the site more often. But the disparities in usage were far greater than one might expect.

Traffic analysis for mid-size newspaper web site

Type of visitor	Number of visitors	Visitors as % of total	Page views	% of total page views	Page views per visitor
Fans	19,661	4.3%	2,820,000	55.8%	143.4
Regulars	13,879	3.1%	430,000	8.5%	30.9
Occasionals	78,292	17.3%	810,000	16.0%	10.3
Fly-bys	341,045	75.3%	998,000	19.7%	2.9
Total	452,877	100%	5,058,000	100%	

SOURCE: Scout Analytics analysis of client's data; name of client is withheld

Fans, despite their small numbers, were responsible for more than 55 percent of the site's traffic. Fly-bys—those people most likely to come from a search engine or a blog—clicked on barely three pages a month. Overall, each fan generated about 50 times more traffic per person than a fly-by.

"When people talk about the size of an audience, that's a sham," Shanahan says. In his view, stated numbers don't reflect how differently the varieties of users act in the way they navigate a site. Publishers mistakenly focus on "page views rather than length of time," he writes on his blog, Digital Equilibrium.[8] Referring to ad "impressions," which are appearances (not clicks) of ads, Shanahan adds, "Using today's standard, there is no difference between impressions that last 1 second, 10 seconds, or 2 minutes."

"The digital world has changed the revenue dynamics for publishers," he adds in another post. "In the print world, a publisher's shipment of physical media was the basis for generating revenue. In the digital world, consumption of media is the basis for revenue. ... In other words, engagement is the unit of monetization."[9]

Shanahan says the benefit of more engagement isn't just in higher ad rates, but in relationships that publishers need to build with their most loyal readers—something that has been lost in the drive to attract mass audiences. By chasing after large audiences rather than deeply engaged ones, he says, news organizations are sacrificing advertising revenue. Publishers who have a "direct relationship with fans can push better contextual advertising"—that is, ads that relate directly to a user's habits and interests. "A publisher can know which fans saw which advertisements in which context on their site." Sites can use that information to provide readers with targeted ads or offers.

And, news organizations that hope to charge for online access need to locate—and cater to—fans, since engaged users are more likely to subscribe. That way of thinking is at the heart of the New York Times' decision to charge for access to its digital editions. The Times built its pay scheme so light users of the site won't have to pay for access, while heavier users—defined as those clicking on at least 20 stories a month—will be charged. But the Times also sees a connection between engagement and advertising. Michael Golden, vice chairman and president of the New York Times Co., discussed the different kinds of online audiences during a speech at a March 2011 advertising conference, shortly before the pay strategy went into effect. Speaking of less committed users, Golden said, "Their engagement is limited, but their numbers are impressive. ... We have to balance engagement and reach. The higher the engagement, the higher the CPM."[10]

*   *   *

Two media outlets with very different editorial missions—Gawker Media and PBS—have tackled this issue of trying to differentiate more and less engaged segments of their audience when pricing advertising.

Gawker's network of sites, started by British journalist Nick Denton in 2003, includes Gizmodo (for gadget lovers), Deadspin (for sports fans) and Jalopnik (for car buffs). In March 2010, Gawker began touting a metric it calls "branded traffic." This was defined as people who have bookmarked the company's sites or arrived at them by searching specifically for the site by name—by, say, typing "Deadspin" into a search engine.[11]

Gawker found that roughly 40 percent of visits come via branded routes, as contrasted to links from search engines. And such visitors are more devoted and engaged, spending 91 seconds more per visit than others. That is a meaningful difference with financial impact, says Erin Pettigrew, Gawker Media's marketing director.

First, the more engaged users are more likely to see highly profitable "roadblock" advertisements—ads that take over the home page of the site for several seconds and then fade away to reveal the editorial content of the page. That revenue helps compensate when advertising rates fall at Gawker and other sites. As Reuters' Felix Salmon has noted, the number of online ads has been growing so fast that advertisers can demand lower rates. As a result, wrote Salmon, "Denton says that since 2008 he has been getting only half the revenue per page that he used to get in 2004."[12]

One way to counteract that is to try to sell more "branding" advertising on the Web—that is, ads designed to draw positive attention to a company's name and image, rather than to trigger a direct response to an offer for a product or service.

Brand advertising has long been profitable for traditional media, especially television and magazines. But because publishers have struggled to convince advertisers that the Web is a good platform for branded ads, they've often missed out on this lucrative revenue stream. "We had been told ad frequency of more than two or three exposures is a bad thing," said Pettigrew. "But for brand advertising, it's different. Six to 12 exposures [of an ad] increased the persuasiveness. And this is the most useful segment to our advertisers."

Because Gawker Media has an array of sites on different topics, it can sell engagement across its network. Thus, the same readers who click on gadget stories at Gizmodo can be served with branded ads at Lifehacker or Gawker. And if Gawker Media can demonstrate to advertisers that its readers are loyal, it can charge higher ad rates, Pettigrew said.

At the other end of cultural spectrum, the Public Broadcasting System's Web strategists are also using engagement metrics to increase revenue.

Amy Sample, director of web analytics for PBS Interactive, says she and others at the site modified a formula created by Web analysts Eric Peterson and Joseph Carrabis to get a better sense of which readers were most devoted.[13] They came up with their own criteria to determine PBS.org's most loyal audience, based on the number of pages a reader views, the amount of time a reader spends on the site, and how often and how recently readers have come.

As it turned out, less than 5 percent of the visits on the site came from users who met all of PBS's engagement standards. But those people are a critical group, says Sample. She found that they stay on PBS.org for 13.5 minutes per visit (compared with a three-minute average for everyone else) and click on nine pages per visit (versus three for other users). PBS saw economic benefits from this audience. Such users were 38 percent more likely to donate money to PBS than less engaged users; they were also more prone to encourage others to use the site. And when PBS saw the usage patterns, executives decided that video, a favorite platform for frequent users, should be promoted more prominently. That translated into revenue, because the site's video ads get healthy $30 CPMs, Sample said, or about three times as high as other ads on the site.

*   *   *

Engagement correlates with editorial content. To see how the relationship plays out at a large site, we can examine some numbers for dallasnews.com, the main site for the Dallas Morning News. (These metrics are from the full year of 2010, a few months before the publisher began charging for access to much of the site.)

For the year, the site averaged around 40 million page views a month, driven by 5 million visitors who visit, on average, about twice a month and click on about four pages per visit. Those numbers are fairly typical for a site the size of Dallas' and provided the publisher, James Moroney, some of the figures he used to calculate the rationale for instituting the pay-for-access plan (see Chapter 5).

But the broad numbers tell only part of the story. In fact, dallasnews.com, like many big online organizations, is many sites rolled into one. To analyze its data, the company sorts its traffic statistics into various categories, including by content areas: news, entertainment, sports, weather and blogs.

News gets the most traffic, in terms of total visitors and visits. News visitors average around two visits a month and click on an average of about 1.5 pages per visit. Their habits are typical of those found at many other news sites—not particularly engaged.

Sports does better in engagement. Users average about 2.3 visits a month, and about 3.4 pages per visit over the course of the year. During the fall of 2010, when the Texas Rangers were in the Major League Baseball playoffs and the Dallas Cowboys were on the football field, users clicked on four or more pages per visit.

And then there's a feature on the site called High School GameTime, which includes rosters, schedules and results from the state where "Friday Night Lights" is based. Users clicked on nearly nine pages per visit in November 2010, during the height of the football season, and generated almost as many page views as the entire news section. Over the year, high school sports fans were about five times as engaged as the people coming to read news.

It's easy to see why. The site offers a dizzying array of statistics, rosters and standings for more than 200 high schools in the Dallas-Fort Worth area. Mark Francescutti, senior managing online editor for sports, says the site's engagement demonstrates the power of "great local content … that is exclusive and is important to people." And loyalty, not search engine optimization, is the key to maintaining the audience. "We might get lucky and get linked off Google, but we want people who will come back every single day," he says.

The site has a small but intense crew. The News' four full-time high school sports reporters file frequently, and editors also rely on clerks who take scores and statistics over the phone from stringers around Dallas. On Friday nights, scores are updated during games, not just reported when the games are over.

Several sites in one at Dallasnews.com

	Monthly pages per visitor
News	2.78
Weather	4.83
Entertainment	2.50
Sports	7.71
High School GameTime	14.07

Data shown are monthly averages for 2010.
SOURCE: Dallas Morning News internal traffic reports

There's also a live chat where reporters update games—"controlled chaos," in the words of Kyle Whitfield, the site's editor. High School GameTime aggregates heavily from other sources. "Our writers are not robots," says Francescutti. "We don't have that old journalistic ego that says, 'If we didn't write it, it's not important.' "

The News used High School Game-Time as part of a package deal with Time Warner Cable that also included print ads, a radio show, a player-of-the-week contest and a banquet at the end of the football season. High School GameTime has brought in up to $700,000, says Richard Alfano, a general manager. For the next season, he says, the News will sell a $1.99 mobile app for High School GameTime that will include play-by-play from at least 100 games a week.

The key, says Whitfield, is focusing on something that readers care about deeply and that no other news provider does as well. "It's more difficult to sell Cowboys coverage, because Cowboys fans are everywhere around the country," Whitfield said. "We were able to organize our resources and monetize it, which is oh-so-rare online."

*   *   *

Rapid audience growth is often accompanied by thin engagement. Such has been the case at Examiner.com, a freelance-driven site that has built an audience of more than 22 million unique users in three years.

Examiner is owned by Clarity Digital Group, which is controlled by Philip Anschutz, a Denver entrepreneur who has made billions in energy, railroads, entertainment and sports franchises. The site, which was started in April 2008, has brought aboard more than 72,000 freelancers who have written on topics ranging from roses in Rhode Island to parenting in Portland.[14] There's not a great deal of supervision: Writers must pass a criminal background check, and they get some quick training. Their first story goes through an editor, but after that, the writers usually post directly to the site.

Page views are a key factor in determining writers' pay, which amounts to between $1 and $7.50 per thousand views, according to AdAge, or a few dollars per article.[15] According to Mike Noe, senior director of recruiting, fewer than a third of the writers are currently "active," which, in Examiner parlance, means they've posted something to the site within the last 90 days.

The content that Examiner.com produces mimics much of what has traditionally appeared in the back of newspapers or at the end of broadcasts—subjects like sports, weather, hobbies or opinion. Writers are hired in large part based on their zeal for a topic. "In a traditional newspaper, the reporter might not be passionate about the [Denver] Broncos," says Jen Nestel, Examiner's director of community. "We do the reverse. We take someone who is already passionate and we teach them how to write." The site doesn't claim to replace the newsgathering functions of traditional media: "Finding out how the school board works is hard," says Rick Blair, chief executive officer of Examiner.com. "It takes a special kind of digger. I could see other folks using platforms like ours to do that. But we don't have the tools or the accredited manpower."

For all its success in building an audience, Examiner has quite low engagement: Its readers see about 65 million page views a month, or only about three pages per visitor. That is likely tied to the site's dependence on search engine optimization, or SEO.

"The problem with SEO is, the visitors are snackers," says Blair. "If people come in through the front door [the home page], they read seven to eight pages. If they come in the side door [such as a search engine], they read maybe two," he says. Suzie Austin, senior vice president for content and marketing, adds, "From the very beginning, we did search engine optimization right. The benefit is obvious—you get a lot of eyeballs. The downside is, there's not a lot of engagement. Page views per user is growing, but at a low rate." And as sites use SEO to boost traffic, advertisers take advantage of the flood of page views around the Web to "name their price," says Tom Woerner, Examiner's senior vice president for national sales. There are two ways for publishers to deal with that, he says: "Play the price game, or add value to what you give the advertiser."

So Examiner is shifting from simply selling display ads to selling the value of its ability to project stories beyond the confines of its own site. Examiner coaches its writers on deploying social media to broaden the influence of their stories. In the marketing business, using social networks is now considered a form of "earned media"—that is, it's more akin to publicity, like an appearance in a news article, than to an advertisement or paid product placement. "Thirty years ago, if you got a story into Sports Illustrated about your product, that was 'earned' media because you didn't pay for it," says Woerner. Today, earned media includes messages that go out via Facebook, Twitter and blogs. "Marketers have to be willing to give up a little control." Woerner also said, "The key for traditional media is how they're engaging with their audience. They got used to the role of the gatekeeper. They need to invite the audience in."

To attract ads from Iams, Procter & Gamble's pet-food company, for example, Examiner invited (but didn't require) its writers who focus on animals to write about pet adoption and shelters; just as importantly, editors encouraged writers to distribute their stories via social networks. Iams didn't control the content, but given how innocuous the Examiner's coverage of animals tends to be, the company was unlikely to be troubled by photo galleries of adorable homeless puppies and feature articles about courageous German shepherds.[16] About 840 writers responded with more than 5,200 articles and additional posts on social-media sites linking back to the stories. Those extra links from Facebook and Twitter to Examiner stories helped drive up advertising rates. Site executives say that ads sold in this effort get CPMs of more than $11, as contrasted to their usual display ads that get CPMs of $3 to $5.

Most other online news organizations are also establishing fan pages on Facebook, setting up Twitter feeds and encouraging readers to share links. They are doing this not just because the networks are where the audiences are, but because they think social media will bring readers who are more engaged than those who come through search engines. At Gawker, Google-driven traffic "is waning," says Pettigrew, the marketing director. Facebook is now the top referrer, and Twitter is gaining. But it wasn't easy for Gawker management to come to terms with social media. "We didn't want to join in the 'fan-page game,'" she said, lest readers become more accustomed to accessing its stories from Facebook than from Gawker's home pages. "You want to own the distribution." But eventually, Facebook's power as a traffic-driver won out. "You can't ignore the way people want to access content."

Vadim Lavrusik, former community manager at social media site Mashable, says that "readers who come through social are far different in their behaviors. They tend to view more articles on average and stick around the site longer." Facebook and Twitter visitors spent 29 percent more time on Mashable.com, he said, and viewed 20 percent more pages than visitors arriving via search engines.

Similarly, at The Atlantic's website, "The percentage of referrals from social nets is coming in at about 15 percent. And it's growing," says Scott Havens, vice president of digital strategy and operations. There's a wide array of social sharing tools on TheAtlantic.com, including Facebook, Twitter, Digg and Reddit. The Atlantic has also started using Tumblr, a microblogging platform that allows anyone—from individuals to media companies—to post text, photos and videos. It has a distinctive visual format and is another way to drive engaged traffic. Newsweek.com also uses Tumblr, including links to a wide variety of sources. By doing that, the magazine can "introduce people to Newsweek who would never read it" on its site or in print, says Mark Coatney, who worked at Newsweek before joining Tumblr in 2010. And he says that while Newsweek's Tumblr audience is smaller than the audience it gets through Twitter or Facebook, its readers are more engaged.

* * *

The argument about whether it's more important to build large audiences or engaged audiences has not been settled. Two news organizations that haven't jumped on the engagement bandwagon are New York Magazine and Newser. "The notion of engagement has been touted for a number of years," says Michael Silberman, general manager of nymag.com. "This is not important in driving our business. We want to grow uniques"—that is, the number of users—"so we're really thinking about the scale. Secondarily, we want to drive page views." He might change his mind if nymag.com decided to start charging for online access, but that isn't on the table for now. "Engagement only makes sense in a subscription model," he says.

At Newser, an aggregator with about 2.5 million unique visitors a month, the audience breaks down in ways similar to mainstream news organizations. Executive Chairman Patrick Spain says about 12,000 users are "addicted" and come to the site many times a day; 225,000 are "avid" users who visit Newser many times a week; and more than 2 million people pass by, with just a click or two. But Spain argues that the passers-by are useful, because they are more likely than addicted users to click on ads, though whether clicks on ads are a good indicator of value is an open question.[17]

* * *

For decades, many news organizations enjoyed higher profits dependent largely on bigger audiences. Magazines and newspapers priced their wares artificially low to boost circulation, even though that brought a group of lightly affiliated readers who had to be lured again and again with cheap come-ons and giveaways. When this worked economically, it was because advertisers could be persuaded to buy access to a big audience they didn't know much about. Today, advertisers have far more choices and far more information. Moreover, many of the firms competing for ad dollars never would have been defined as "media companies" years ago. Facebook now delivers almost a quarter of all digital advertising views in the U.S.[18] Search advertising, dominated by Google, soaks up almost half the dollars spent on online ads.[19]

So it is much harder for media companies, new or old, to compete purely on audience size. They will never grow fast enough to counter the massive numbers accumulated by giants like Google and Facebook. News organizations have to offer something more.

When the New York Times announced details of its digital subscription plan in March 2011, Andrew Swinand, president of global operations for the Starcom MediaVest Group, a media-buying agency, said it wouldn't hurt—and might help—the site's advertising revenue.[20] "I'm paying for an engaged audience, and if that audience is willing to pay, that demonstrates just how engaged they are," he said. In a later interview, he added that editors need to start thinking about engagement in broader terms, not just the amount of time people spend on a site or the number of pages they click. "I want to be able to look and say, 'Who are these people [using a site], and what are they spending their time doing on it?' " By doing that, Swinand says, news organizations can help companies feel more confident that their ad dollars are being spent wisely. The Times' Golden adds that "if we all go the way of outdoor advertising [e.g., billboards] where it depends on who passes by, it'll be hard to build value. Engagement is the proxy by which people value content."

Audience size is still vitally important. A site with 10 million unique users will get more attention from advertisers and agencies than one with a fifth that many. Large companies want to make mass purchases of ads; they won't deal individually with a host of small sites. But the chase for traffic has put news organizations on a sugar high of fat audiences and thin revenue. It has also devalued their journalism, as they have resorted to such tactics as celebrity photo slideshows to boost search-driven traffic. In diminishing their brands and commoditizing their content, they have fallen short in the crucial goal of attracting engaged, loyal users. This needs to change. By producing relevant journalism, deploying data intelligently, and relying on social media—not just search engines—to drive traffic, they can gather a more devoted and involved readership, one that advertisers will also prefer.

---

[1] In its results for the second quarter of 2010, http://bit.ly/h31e8V, the Times Co. says 26 percent of its total ad revenue comes from online. But for the New York Times Media Group, which includes the namesake property and the International Herald Tribune (print and online), circulation revenue is almost as significant as advertising. Thus, digital certainly represents less than 20 percent of total revenue for the NYT's paper and site, though the company doesn't break the results out in more detail.

[2] "Morgan Stanley's Meeker Sees Online Ad Boom," Bloomberg Businessweek, Nov. 16, 2010. http://buswk.co/dP8wQU (full presentation available at http://slidesha.re/dHqdrC). A March 2011 study by eMarketer, http://bit.ly/htZ3Mw, put the time spent vs. ad spending disparity at 25.2 vs. 18.7 percent for Internet and 8.1 vs. 0.5 percent for mobile.

[3] According to a comScore study released in March 2011, "Lessons Learned, Maximizing Returns with Digital Media," 30 percent of all U.S. Internet users delete their cookies, up to six times a month. That can result in a 250 percent overcounting of unique visitors to a site. Slide 6 of http://bit.ly/hhIf0y

[4] Jimmy Orr, "Latimes.com Has Record Page Views in March," latimes.com, April 8, 2011. http://lat.ms/i435ob

[5] "Nielsen Analysis," State of the News Media 2010, Pew Research Center's Project for Excellence in Journalism. http://bit.ly/gcIRQ2 The study also notes that the average visitor spends 10 minutes a month on newspaper or local TV sites, while cable news sites get close to 24 minutes per month.

[6] "Newspaper Engagement," submission to Newspaper Association of America Marketing Conference, Feb. 23, 2006. http://bit.ly/i2b6Eg

[7] Scout Analytics is actually measuring devices, not humans, but there is reason to believe the numbers even out in some fashion. Many people use more than one device in a month to access a site, but also some devices, especially home computers, are used by more than one person in the same period of time.

[8] "Importance of Analyzing Unit Cost of Engagement in Advertising," Digital Equilibrium blog, Nov. 29, 2010. http://bit.ly/ihY3nc

[9] "Engagement as the Unit of Monetization," Digital Equilibrium blog, Oct. 25, 2010. http://bit.ly/ejvcJp

[10] Remarks at Borrell Associates Local Online Advertising Conference, March 3, 2011.

[11] Erin Pettigrew, "Strengthening Our Core (Readership)," Gawker Media, March 5, 2010. http://bit.ly/hnQnLv

[12] Felix Salmon, "The New Gawker Media," Reuters.com, Dec. 1, 2010. http://reut.rs/gBg6lt

[13] Eric Peterson and Joseph Carrabis, "Measuring the Immeasurable: Visitor Engagement," Web Analytics Demystified, 2008. http://bit.ly/hvFuio PBS later adapted the formula to designate its most loyal users as those who view at least 3.2 pages per visit; stay at least 2.57 minutes on the site; have visited the site within the past two weeks; and visit the site at least three times a month.

[14] Examiner articles at http://exm.nr/gZSbnU and http://exm.nr/fl2JEJ

[15] Edmund Lee, "Does Who Creates Content Matter to Marketers in a 'Pro-Am' Media World?", AdAge, June 7, 2010. http://exm.nr/fl2JEJ

[16] Examiner gallery and article at http://exm.nr/fHdRPW and http://exm.nr/eonVdC

[17] Gawker's Nick Denton wrote that "clickthroughs are an indicator of the blindness, senility or idiocy of readers rather than the effectiveness of the ads." From "Why Gawker is moving beyond the blog," Lifehacker blog, Nov. 30, 2010. http://lifehac.kr/gVWcuF For more on the inutility of clicks, see comScore study, op. cit. Slide 4 of http://bit.ly/hhIf0y which reports that 84 percent of all U.S. Internet users never click on an ad in a given month, and that there are 50 percent fewer clickers in 2011 than in 2007.

[18] comScore press release, "U.S. Online Display Advertising Market Delivers 22 Percent Increase in Impressions vs. Year Ago," Nov. 8, 2010. http://bit.ly/ezZAYa

[19] "Online: Key Questions Facing Digital News," State of the News Media 2011, Pew Research Center's Project for Excellence in Journalism. http://bit.ly/gKShzD

[20] Jeremy W. Peters, "The Times Announces Digital Subscription Plan," New York Times, March 17, 2011. http://nyti.ms/gNtUg8

Chapter 3

Local and Niche Sites: *The Advantages of Being Small*

TBD.com ran into trouble right from the start. In February 2011, just six months after going live, the Washington, D.C., area's high-profile experiment in local online journalism announced that it would lay off half of its editorial staff, detach its site from its TV-station partner and reinvent itself as a culture-and-lifestyle site. Many of those who did stay on looked for the exit as soon as they could line up another job.

The reshuffling—which followed the departure of Jim Brady, the former Washington Post online executive brought in to launch the site—marked the meaningful end of one of the best-funded and best-pedigreed efforts to make professional journalism work online. The site, whose name stands for To Be Determined, had drawn a great deal of attention for the quality of its editorial staff and for its use of social media.[1] Clearly there was an important lesson here for other news sites, especially those plying the local or "hyperlocal" trade.

Just what that lesson was, though, is in dispute. Does TBD's failure prove that "hyperlocal journalism is more hype than hope," as media analyst Alan Mutter put it?[2] Or did it mainly signal a failure of nerve on the part of corporate parent Allbritton Communications, whose CEO, Robert Allbritton, had pledged to provide a three- to five-year runway to profitability?

It is clear that the site was, as expected, losing money, despite impressive traffic growth. According to coverage in the Washington Post, unique visitors to TBD.com had risen from 715,000 in November 2010 to 838,000 in December and 1.5 million in January 2011. But, as the incoming head of the site told the paper, "It was still not generating enough [income] to offset the hefty costs."[3] Two insiders interviewed for this report said the January traffic spike was not as striking as it looks, because much of it consisted of people looking for information on the region's heavy snowstorms that month.

Nobody involved has revealed the precise size of TBD's losses. Saul Carlin, an Allbritton executive involved with TBD from the start, would say only that "traffic and revenue were being closely monitored. As a result, a change in management was necessary."

Brady says the picture was not that grim. The site had been budgeted to earn revenue "in the low millions" in year one; he argues it was on track to reach perhaps 75 percent of that goal. "The situation wasn't great when I left, but it wasn't catastrophic either," he says.

Mutter, a former journalist and media executive, took the shortfall as a demonstration of a fundamental misalignment between the expense of producing local reporting and the potential online revenue from it, because of the built-in constraints of small audiences and puny ad rates. Various hyperlocal flameouts support this thesis: among others, the Washington Post's Loudoun Extra and the shuttered New York Times site for suburban New Jersey, whose audience was handed off to local start-up Baristanet.

Still, mistakes were made. Brady has said repeatedly that resistance from the site's broadcast partner WJLA, the Allbritton-owned ABC affiliate in Washington, proved a major hurdle. Both Brady and Steve Buttry, TBD's director of community engagement, said the TV staff was unhappy to see its website rolled into TBD.com—which linked out heavily to other media outlets—and that the station failed to promote TBD wholeheartedly on the air.

"The first time we linked out to another TV site, that was a major collision," says Buttry. He adds that TBD linked out more moderately after that and gave the TV news staff a "heads-up" when it planned to point to a story that WJLA had missed. "The lesson from our experience is that the legacy culture is powerful and ingrained," he says. "Whenever its revenue stream might be endangered or disrupted, it's going to have a big influence on decisions."

The most important example of that influence was the decision to fold TBD's ad sales staff into WJLA's, which led to the departure of the small digital sales team that Brady had assembled. "Selling digital is hard. I was adamant that the only way to be successful was to keep the sales force separate," he says. The tension was visible from the start, Brady adds; an example is an ambitious launch sponsorship of more than $75,000 that his sales team planned to pitch to a local car dealership. WJLA intervened, arguing that it would damage a valuable relationship between the dealer and the TV station, Brady says.

"When I was at the Post, we were routinely doing six-figure online deals," Brady says. "If the sales force itself doesn't believe digital is worth it, how are they going to sell it? To just assume nobody would ever spend that much online is insecurity with your own inventory."

Just as revealing as what went wrong is the list of things TBD seemed to have going for it, which help to clarify the intense interest local online news ventures have drawn for the last five years. Most important was its association with sister site Politico.com, another well-funded, generously staffed Allbritton venture led by high-profile news veterans. Like Politico, TBD promised to be not just on the Web but "of the Web," in Brady's phrase, meaning that it would link abundantly, deploy social media aggressively and engage closely with users. And like Politico, TBD promised to deliver to its advertisers a well-defined audience—not just generic news consumers, but people intensely interested in the particular news it had to offer. (Still, it is worth keeping in mind that at least through 2009, Politico earned more than half its revenue from its free, ad-supported print edition,[4] with a circulation of about 32,000.[5])

TBD also sought to strike a balance between focus and scale: Visitors would be drawn in by news about their immediate environs or interests, but behind the scenes the operation could reap the "efficiencies" of serving a large metropolitan area. (Brady insists "hyperlocal" is the wrong word for what was really a regional site with a neighborhood interface.) Likewise, the site would include a mix of aggregation and firsthand reporting. To describe the site, Robert Allbritton has used the analogy of a supermarket bringing together items that previously could not be found in one place. Before TBD, he declared when the site launched, finding local news online was "like trying to buy groceries in the old country. First you went to the fishmonger, then to the baker, then to the grocer, and so on."[6]

Other hyperlocal ventures have tried to apply versions of that idea on a national scale. A good recent example is Main Street Connect, a "national community news company" that went live in 2009 and consists, so far, of 10 sites serving towns in Fairfield County, Conn. The separate sites share editorial resources (neighboring communities see many of the same articles), technology infrastructure and an ad sales team. "We'll soon be bringing our vision to other groups of towns," Main Street's web site promises. "Watch for us."[7]

By far the grandest of the new hyperlocal journalism ventures is the nationwide Patch network, which was bought by a struggling AOL in 2009. With sites in 700 communities and counting as of March 2011, each led by a local editor making $40,000 to $50,000 a year, Patch has turned AOL into one of the biggest sources of new journalism jobs in the country. Visitors to a local Patch site see news and information about a specific community, written and curated by people in that community, whether it's Dublin, Calif., or Dunedin, Fla. (In March 2011, AOL also bought Outside.in, a hyperlocal network that automatically aggregates news, blog posts, police reports and other public data, and says it is in 57,830 neighborhoods. Reports suggest AOL was interested in the underlying technology more than the business itself.[8])

To run all of those Patch sites, AOL can count on centralized resources like a massive in-house ad network, a sales force with ties to national brands, and sophisticated search engine optimization technology for maximizing the meaningful lifespan—and thus the economic return—of every piece of content it produces. Like McDonald's, AOL uses sophisticated market research to assess the commercial potential of the communities where it is considering planting the Patch flag. (According to a New Yorker profile of AOL chief executive officer Tim Armstrong, the Patch formula considers 59 factors, from average incomes to voter turnout.[9])

The same infrastructure supports AOL's growing stable of niche or "vertical" content sites, anchored by acquisitions such as the martial-arts blog MMAFighting.com, the tech-industry site TechCrunch and the sprawling Huffington Post, which AOL bought for $315 million in 2011. It's no exaggeration to say that AOL, whose original business model (providing dial-up access to the Internet) is badly out of date, has staked its declining fortunes on local and niche journalism.

Why? The underlying logic is the same at AOL as it was at TBD: In a world where much of the daily news has become commodified, only news that people can't find elsewhere will command a loyal audience. This is hardly a novel insight among media analysts, who since the late 1990s have pointed to financial news as a rare example of the sort of information that people, and advertisers, will pay for online.

A 2006 report on "value creation" in journalism, from Harvard's Kennedy School of Government, put the lesson bluntly: "specialize or localize."[10] As the report explained, "Because of the increasing range of information sources, greater abilities to access material from anyplace at anytime, and requirements to create tight bonds that lead to loyal consumers, news organizations will have to move away from the unfocused, something-for-everyone, one-size-fits-no-one news products characteristic of the second half of the twentieth century."

Of course, not every news outlet can be the Financial Times or the Wall Street Journal, with long-cultivated expertise in a valuable and time-sensitive brand of information. For most, the clearest path to "adding value" lies in paying closer attention to their immediate community. The Harvard report put this drily: "To be competitive and create economic value, media will need to increase their differentiation, and thus exclusivity. The most effective way to do so is to create value through local coverage that is linked to the lives, aspirations, and understanding of individuals in the locations in which they live. It is this kind of coverage that other news providers cannot do well."

That's the theory. But TBD, Patch, the hyperlocal sites launched by the New York Times and the Washington Post, and many others like them have yet to produce a commercially viable proof-of-concept. The list of success stories in local online news hasn't changed much in recent years; it contains mainly small, grass-roots community sites. If nonprofit ventures with significant foundation funding, such as MinnPost and the Voice of San Diego, are removed from the list, most of what's left are Baristanet, Alaska Dispatch, The Batavian, West Seattle Blog and a few others.

These ventures vary in their business models and the kind of journalism they produce. What they have in common is limited resources, a narrow coverage footprint and no claim to the corporate efficiencies of their larger peers.

* * *

Alaska Dispatch is a statewide news site launched in 2008 by the husband-and-wife reporting team of Tony Hopfinger and Amanda Coyne. In 2009, philanthropist and former *U.S. News & World Report* executive Alice Rogoff bought a majority share; the founders stayed on as editors, and the Dispatch was relaunched with a mandate to build up a newsroom and dedicate itself to serious political journalism.

Today the site has a full-time editorial and Web staff of 10, up from just two at launch. It also uses paid freelancers. Total staff costs run in the neighborhood of $650,000 per year. The Dispatch saves money by avoiding print and delivery costs, which is an especially serious expense for dailies in Alaska. In late 2008 the Dispatch's print rival, the Anchorage Daily News, ended rural air delivery to the state's remote outposts.

Rogoff says the Dispatch doesn't stint on the costs of covering the Alaskan frontier. The newsroom is attached to an airplane hangar in Anchorage, and access to Rogoff's airplane has made it easier to cover distant events like the Iditarod sled race. (The Dispatch also drew praise for its reporting on the 2008 Point Hope caribou massacre and subsequent trial.[11]) Tony Hopfinger says the site focuses on statewide political news and analysis—exactly what many small dailies have cut in favor of covering murders and car wrecks.

The site's founders say that commercial success is integral to the mission of the Alaska Dispatch. Even the "About Us" page repeats the message: "Because the owners of the Alaska Dispatch believe that journalism must and will ultimately pay for itself, the site is a for-profit enterprise, relying on online advertising and sponsorship." When she became publisher, Rogoff committed to backing the site until it turns a profit, which she expected to happen in three years. Now, about two years in, she won't disclose financial details but says the Dispatch is on track to meet its goals.

The Dispatch does appear to have found a niche in Alaska's news ecosystem. Roughly 125,000 unique visitors generate more than 1 million page views each month, impressive statistics in a state of just over 700,000 inhabitants. According to Hopfinger, the site has about 30 to 40 advertisers at a time; its ad rates run from $150 to $1,550 per month, with a guaranteed minimum of 75,000 impressions. Though pricing is by the month, the site will oblige advertisers who would rather buy by the amount of traffic—hence the guarantee. And the Dispatch's modest entry-level rates compare favorably with print alternatives.

One of the Dispatch's biggest challenges has been to forecast the amount of ad space, or inventory, it will have each month, because this fluctuates greatly depending on how much traffic the site gets. On occasion, the site has had to turn advertisers away. To deepen and diversify its inventory without taking on too much risk in increased editorial costs, Hopfinger plans to bring established Alaskan blogs into the Dispatch under a revenue-sharing agreement.

At first glance, the statewide profile of the Dispatch seems to set it apart from smaller local sites. But Rogoff and Hopfinger stress that Alaska's agenda-setters constitute a kind of village, one spread among Anchorage, Juneau, Washington and Houston. They share a narrow and well-defined set of interests: federal funding, government regulation, the oil industry (hence the Houston link), transportation, Sarah Palin and so on. One of the site's most successful features is its "Bush Pilot" blog, focused on the small-scale aviation so critical to Alaskan life.

"It's like a small town," Hopfinger says. "The flipside of that is there are fewer people and fewer businesses." But he adds that the Dispatch has benefited from the kind of boosterism that smaller community sites enjoy. "You get an opportunity as an underdog. People want to see us succeed," he says.

An emphasis on a small and well-defined community sets apart most of the online-only local news outlets that began to dot the Web about five years ago. These run, generally, from professionally staffed hard-news outlets such as the Dispatch to news-oriented community blogs like Baristanet and West Seattle Blog. Wherever each site falls along that spectrum, none of these grass-roots ventures has either the assets or the built-in costs of local sites backed by established newspapers or television stations. (For a detailed discussion of costs, see Chapter 7.)

The grass-roots sites also face a different set of problems than do large-scale, networked hyperlocal ventures such as Patch, and, to a lesser extent, the original TBD. Patch is hardly a legacy newsroom. But it does have to succeed on a scale that justifies AOL's vast editorial, infrastructural and ad-sales investments (and that compensates for the company's declining income as an Internet service provider.) If only a few of the 700-plus Patch sites take root and thrive in their communities, that won't be enough for the enterprise to succeed; for the business to make sense, the bulk of them have to work.

Landscape of local online news

Local and "hyperlocal" news sites vary both in their coverage footprint and in their affiliation with traditional print or broadcast outlets. Many of the success stories in online journalism appear in the bottom left quadrant: small, grass-roots ventures without corporate backing or ties to established newsrooms.

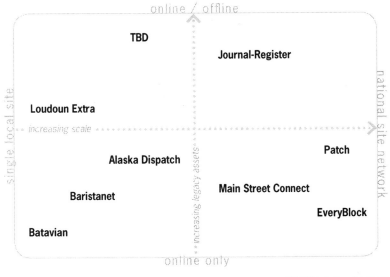

SOURCE: Authors' analysis

These distinctions suggest two axes for plotting the local news ventures working online, depicted in the chart shown here. The vertical axis distinguishes online-only outlets from those that also have traditional print or broadcast assets. The horizontal axis arrays organizations according to their editorial footprint: single-site, hyperlocal outlets covering a community or neighborhood; sites or small site networks covering a cluster of communities; and site networks with a regional or national scale.

The local news sites on the top half the chart are tied to substantial legacy operations, whether they are based in one city or spread across a chain of newsrooms that share back-end resources. These sites enjoy the same advantage in serving their local audiences that the New York Times site does in delivering national news online: access to the editorial resources of established professional newsrooms. But that editorial product published online yields only a tiny fraction of the ad revenue that it does in print or broadcast. The health of these sites is effectively wedded to the health of their traditional parents.

The hyperlocal networks in the bottom right quadrant don't have legacy newsrooms to draw on. They must either build an editorial staff from scratch, like Patch and Main Street Connect, or cull local information from public sources and other sites, as do EveryBlock (now owned by MSNBC) and Outside.in. Their key asset lies, potentially, in uniting hundreds or thousands of hyperlocal channels with back-end infrastructure for selling and serving advertising.

It is easy to understand the argument that these networks ought to occupy the sweet spot for hyperlocal news. Like a stable of trade publications or a chain of small newspapers, Patch can pull together a large audience out of many small ones. Its size should confer advantages unavailable to local competitors in the individual markets where it operates: lower costs, better technology, access to bigger advertisers and so on. And as noted above, those markets have been carefully selected for their commercial potential.

The bottom left quadrant is the source of the most surprising lessons about building commercially viable journalism online. The independent, locally grown news sites that populate this quadrant would seem to be at a clear disadvantage. They lack the editorial backing from established newsrooms that many competitors enjoy. Their infrastructure costs—bandwidth, content management, ad serving and so on—are fixed and cannot be shared across a network. They lack what has been considered a crucial element of success in the media business: scale.

That several of these grass-roots sites have nevertheless built viable businesses raises two questions. The most obvious one is how they have managed to make ad revenue align with expenses. But just as important—and perhaps still to be determined—is whether their model can support serious accountability journalism.

*   *   *

The city of Batavia, N.Y., is unlikely to show up on AOL's carefully calculated list of promising Patch sites. It is a Rust Belt community of just 16,000 people in the western end of the state, about 50 miles from Buffalo. The prison system is one of the few growth sectors in what was once a thriving industrial center, and Batavia's downtown merchants have struggled to compete with big-box retailers.

When The Batavian's website went live in May 2008, the local paper, the Batavia Daily News (owned by the Johnson Newspaper Corp.) didn't have a website. (It does now.) Gatehouse Media, which publishes small dailies, weeklies and "shoppers" around the country, launched The Batavian as an experiment in online-only publishing. In addition to hiring two reporters, who are no longer there, Gatehouse provided its in-house digital guru, Howard Owens, who became the new site's publisher. In early 2009 Gatehouse laid Owens off and he assumed ownership of The Batavian, which runs as an independent site with no editorial or business ties to other publications.

Three years after going live, The Batavian, according to Owens, is profitable. It offers a promising example of local online journalism. The site has grown from fewer than 2,000 unique visitors per day in 2008 to roughly 6,000 now, generating close to 600,000 page views each month. Owens won't say what it costs to run, but The Batavian operates with a skeleton staff: Owens, his wife, and two part-time employees, in addition to freelancers who are paid a small sum per story. The site posts about five short reported stories per day, and additional bulletins or photo pieces.

Most impressively, The Batavian has about 100 advertisers at any time—up from just three in 2008—and pulled in between $100,000 and $150,000 in ad revenue in 2010, Owens says. He aims to double ad income in 2011 and to hire one or two full-time employees. "I don't really have to sell anymore—they call me," he says of local advertisers. "It's driven by word of mouth."

One factor driving that word of mouth is The Batavian's modest advertising rates. The site eschews pricing by traffic completely; instead it charges a flat fee of $40 to $260 per month (though one premium package runs as high as $400).

Owens estimates that a month's run on his site would buy just one day's placement in his print competitor, the Daily News. "I wanted it to be an easy decision," he says. "What's another $200?"

Online, of course, the supply of space available to sell to advertisers increases with traffic, because "impressions" are the unit of measurement. A small site like The Batavian would be hard-pressed to support 100 advertisers with the top-of-page banner model used by many large metro dailies. With one major banner per page, each sponsor would get just 6,000 impressions per month, or $30 worth at a fairly generous $5 cost-per-thousand. (In 2010 comScore found[12] that average newspaper CPMs were $7 nationwide, though its analysis included the largest newspapers and newspaper chains in the country; small local outlets tend to have lower rates.) At that rate, the site would earn $36,000 a year. If there were two big banners on each page, annual revenue would rise to $72,000.

Instead, Owens runs the site like a "pennysaver"—every advertiser appears on each page, in long columns running down both sides of the site. Their positions rotate during the day to make sure every merchant spends some time near the top. And to encourage scrolling, every article appears in full on the site's front page, with the most recent items at the top. It is possible to absorb all of the day's news without ever clicking beyond the home page. Owens doesn't have to worry about driving traffic to various corners of the site to deliver impressions to different advertisers. He designed this approach based on his experience at three newspaper companies, with access to online data for more than 100 local papers. "I saw that it's very hard to get people to move past the home page," he explains. "So I decided to base my business on that."

A national brand probably would not place its ad alongside 100 others. But Batavia's merchants have the sense that they are sponsoring a popular local resource at a reasonable price. Local boosterism makes a difference, Owens insists: "Some advertisers just want to support community." His advertisers rarely ask about click-through rates, though Owens says some are pleased to learn that, say, a total of 80 people clicked on their ad over the course of a month.

A useful metric for evaluating this approach is not CPM, but RPM—revenue per 1,000 impressions. Assuming The Batavian earned $125,000 in 2010 (the middle of the range Owens claims) and averaged 600,000 page views per month, it achieved an RPM of $17, an impressive figure for a news site serving a small and far-from-affluent community.

*   *   *

A similar formula applies at Baristanet, one of the most successful local news sites in the country. Baristanet has one decisive advantage: its audience of affluent, media-savvy professionals in the retail-rich bedroom communities of suburban New Jersey, anchored by the towns of Montclair and Maplewood. (The area scores well on AOL's algorithms—six of the seven towns Baristanet serves have their own Patch sites.)

Baristanet, launched in 2004, keeps costs radically low. Everyone involved with the site has another job—even the two founders, Liz George and Debbie Galant. "Everyone's freelance," George explains. She and Galant act as top editors, giving the final word on every article; one other editor is paid by the month. The rest of the site's dozen or so freelancers—many of whom moonlight from salaried jobs—are paid by the piece, usually about $50 each. "We don't want long articles," George says. "If they spend half the day on a story, that's too long."

Then there are people who write for free, submitting opinion pieces, comments, bulletins and photos. Baristanet offers roughly the mix of content that a community weekly would; one Friday in March 2011, for instance, some political news about local budgets was sandwiched between pieces on "weekend highlights" for kids and a major markdown at the local cheesemonger. George explains that many smaller items require no reporting at all, just a photo and a blurb. The combination of paid articles, opinion, aggregation, and "things that come in over the transom," yields more than enough material to keep the site fresh, she says.

Altogether, editorial costs run to $5,000 or $6,000 per month—higher than at The Batavian, but still fairly modest for a site that runs about eight longer articles per day and, according to George, attracts 80,000 unique visitors monthly. Most important, costs are far below the roughly $20,000 in advertising that George says Baristanet pulls in each month. For several years, according to George, the site's profits have provided a sizable second income for the two founders and their hired editor.

Baristanet also eschews cost-per-thousand pricing in favor of a simple calendar model, and, though rates run higher than at the Batavian, an advertiser can get on the site quite cheaply. Merchants pay from $150 to $1,600 per month (weekly rates are also available) depending on their ad's size, placement and frequency of rotation. George says businesses in the area have no interest in buying by the impression or by the click, though Baristanet does report such statistics to them.

Because Baristanet rotates ads across its available inventory, a merchant's exposure is limited by the amount of traffic the site gets. According to George, consultants have advised against ad rotation, but so far the hospitals, car dealerships, real estate agents, restaurants and other businesses that advertise on the site don't seem to mind. Merchants occasionally call wondering where their ad is; George advises them to refresh the page a few times until it appears.

As a result, Baristanet achieves an enviable ratio of revenue to traffic. With an average monthly volume of about 475,000 page views, the site enjoys an RPM in the neighborhood of $42—many times the revenue it would get if it used a standard CPM model. Just as The Batavian's revenue would collapse if merchants complained about being stacked together on a single page, Baristanet could not do the business it does each month if it had to guarantee a hard number of impressions to each advertiser.

It seems fair to assume that the site's appeal to advertisers is not tied to such narrow statistics. George suggests that merchants are paying relatively little to be a part of a one-of-a-kind community resource that enjoys wide recognition in the towns it serves. Baristanet claims to have 53 percent household penetration in its core market of Montclair and has logged more than 300,000 comments since its inception—roughly one for every other person in all of Essex County(though many come from repeat commenters). "It's been an easy sell," George says. "Everybody wants to partner with us."

*   *   *

That local online journalism can succeed in such different environments— prosperous suburban New Jersey and Rust Belt upstate New York—is an indication that it can be viable elsewhere. A 2010 survey of 66 "promising local news sites" around the country, conducted by the Reynolds Journalism Institute at the University of Missouri, found that the top objective of these sites was to "produce original news" and that on average nearly half of their content came from paid staff, rather than, for instance, aggregation or reader contributions. [13]

Advertising was far and away the most important revenue source for these sites, accounting for 45 percent of revenue on average. (Foundation grants came next, at 17 percent of revenue, and reader donations followed at 12 percent.) For 28 of the sites surveyed, advertising supplied three-fourths or more of annual revenue. Fifty-six percent of the sites operated as for-profit ventures, and of these, half reported making a profit the previous year. (It is important to remember these results are entirely self-reported.)

Clear lessons emerge from the experiences of Baristanet, The Batavian and the Alaska Dispatch. First, all three sites have embraced calendar-based advertising pricing systems that yield more revenue than they could expect pricing strictly by the number of impressions. Low prices, anecdotal successes and a sense of community engagement allow local merchants to find value on terms that a national advertiser might reject out of hand. The sites have managed to appeal to local advertisers by selling in terms that work for them. "A lot of advertisers don't understand CPMs," says Victor Wong, CEO of PaperG, a company that helps publishers attract local ads. "They don't understand what a page view means, they don't know when the page ran, they don't trust CPM measurement."

But it would be a mistake to see in these examples a formula that any local venture could replicate just by asking merchants for a few hundred dollars each month. Each of these sites filled a vacuum when it launched and has remained popular even as new competitors have appeared. Their real feat is having built sizable audiences on the cheap. The same is true of niche or "vertical" sites that aim for a particular demographic segment or "community of interest," rather than a geographic area.

Henry Blodget's Business Insider (reviewed in detail in Chapter 7) offers a good example: The financial news site reached break-even last year by building a monthly audience of 6 million unique visitors, on a yearly budget of about $5 million. An even more dramatic example is DailyCandy, the decade-old trend-surfing email newsletter that occupies roughly the same journalistic space online that Lucky magazine does in the print world.

DailyCandy was launched in March 2000 from the kitchen table of Dany Levy, then a young editorial-side veteran of New York magazine and Lucky. Levy's venture offered one of the most bare-bones editorial propositions imaginable: a short daily email alerting readers to something hot—a new cupcake shop, a shoe style—in New York's (and the Internet's) fast-changing retail culture.

"One simple thing in your e-mail inbox that told you one thing you needed to do that day," Levy explained to a Harvard Business Review blog in 2009. "It was meant to save people time and keep them plugged in. Not everyone can afford to eat at Mario Batali's new place, or some other hot, new restaurant, but this kind of knowledge is cultural currency. It's water-cooler conversation." [14]

That interview came after her company had been bought by Comcast, in the summer of 2008, for a reported $125 million. By the time of the sale, Daily-Candy had grown from a one-person shop to a company with 55 employees, running 12 editions across the country and reaching a total audience of 2.5 million people—most of them women, and two-thirds of them younger than 35. Financial details were scarce, but an internal email from early investor (and veteran of MTV and AOL) Bob Pittman reportedly said the company would reach $25 million in revenue in 2008, with profits of $10 million.[15] Analysts had been speculating eagerly about what the company might be worth since 2006, when the Wall Street Journal reported it was on the auction block at $100 million.[16]

Those numbers put DailyCandy in a different league financially from the local news ventures profiled in this chapter. But the dynamic that makes DailyCandy work was visible years earlier, when the newsletter was a grass-roots venture with much smaller ambitions. Levy launched her business with $50,000 in savings and $250,000 raised from family and friends. The first edition went out to just 700 people, mostly friends or colleagues of Levy, then readership grew explosively. In 2001 the newsletter was already paying for itself, with tiny ads in each emailed edition as well as separate sponsored emails straight from advertisers.

By 2003 the subscriber list had grown to 285,000—more than 400 times its starting audience, a stunning ratio for so-called organic growth achieved with minimal outside support. It was on the basis of these numbers that Pittman made his initial investment in the business, reported to be "in the single-digit millions," which in turn fueled the newsletter's expansion into new markets and new editions. [17]

In a broad sense, the experience of successful local and niche sites bears out the received wisdom that media ventures in today's hypercompetitive landscape must "specialize or localize." But only a fraction of online news outlets that pursue this strategy ultimately succeed. Defining and attracting a desirable audience is necessary, of course, but not by itself sufficient; acquiring that audience on a tight budget is what sets successful grass-roots ventures apart from the also-rans.

---

[1] See, for instance, Laura McGann, "Six reasons to watch local news project TBD's launch next week," Nieman Journalism Lab, Aug. 6, 2010. http://bit.ly/dRnAxQ

[2] Alan D. Mutter, "Hyperlocals like TBD: More hype than hope," Reflections of a Newsosaur, Feb. 24, 2011. http://bit.ly/fVi6M0

[3] Paul Farhi, "Allbritton Communications slashes staff at reorganized TBD.com," Washington Post, Feb. 23, 2011. http://wapo.st/g8XcRa

[4] Rafat Ali, "Politico Crushing It On Revs, Profits In Fiscal '09; Changes Ownership Structure," paidcontent.org, Jan. 4, 2010. http://bit.ly/eMimy7

[5] Michael Wolff, "Politico's Washington Coup," Vanity Fair, August 2009. http://bit.ly/eyx79Y

[6] Paul Farhi, "TBD.com making its move into the crowded market of local news," Washington Post, Aug. 7, 2010. http://wapo.st/hTwEAG

[7] Main Street Connect, "Community News." http://bit.ly/e4nfiB

[8] David Kaplan, "AOL Buying Hyperlocal News Aggregator Outside.in; Will Align With Patch," paidcontent.org, March 4, 2011. http://bit.ly/fZBjsA; and Dan Frommer, "AOL Buys Outside. In, Less Than $10 Million," Business Insider, March 4, 2011. http://read.bi/eBKRaJ

[9] Ken Auletta, "You've Got News," New Yorker, Jan. 24, 2011. http://nyr.kr/eLd7Qn

[10] Robert G. Picard, "Journalism, Value Creation and the Future of News Organizations," Joan Shorenstein Center on the Press, Politics and Public Policy, Spring 2006. http://bit.ly/ep2ufT

[11] David Saleh Rauf, "Dispatches from the Last Frontier," American Journalism Review, December/January 2011. http://bit.ly/fpMpLF

[12] comScore, "The New York Times Ranks as Top Online Newspaper According to May 2010 U.S. comScore Media Metrix Data," June 16, 2010. http://bit.ly/ecqJ37

[13] Michele McLellan, "Block by Block: Building a new news ecosystem," Reynolds Journalism Institute. http://bit.ly/kIjVwv

[14] Anthony Tjan, "DailyCandy's Accidental Entrepreneur: An Interview with Dany Levy," Harvard Business Review, Oct. 14, 2009. http://bit.ly/fmnRzD

[15] Peter Kafka, "Comcast Buys DailyCandy For $125 Million," Business Insider, Aug. 5, 2008. http://read.bi/fg6zNh

[16] Dennis K. Berman and Julia Angwin, "Former AOL Official Pittman Puts Web Firm Daily Candy Up for Sale," Wall Street Journal, Feb. 15, 2006. http://on.wsj.com/gRMprr

[17] Anthony Tjan, op.cit.

Chapter 4

The New New Media: *Mobile, Video and Other Emerging Platforms*

News organizations can be forgiven for feeling that they're in an endless cycle of Whac-A-Mole.

They've had 15 years to get onto the Internet, and for much of that time the experience was limited largely to words and photos on a Web page, accessed on a personal computer. But more recently, journalism has been blessed and bedeviled by a stream of follow-on innovations. As a result, most organizations have tried to develop new ways to report and distribute stories, and many are making substantial investments so their work will appear on attractive new devices. Their hope is that these new kinds of digital journalism will enhance companies' earnings; their fear is that if they don't adapt, they will lose audiences' attention and the revenue it brings.

It hasn't been easy. Video has been seen as a great way to get more sustained engagement, but many news organizations have found it to be expensive and difficult to produce. And even though ad rates are three to five times what regular display ads bring, video often doesn't get enough traffic to attract substantial revenue. Mobile devices, meanwhile, provide consumers with greater access to news, but the small screen size can be a nightmare for designers and a poor display space for advertisers. Tablets—particularly the iPad—have looked like a more immersive experience for readers, and a more likely venue for subscriptions and higher ad revenue. But their luster has dimmed as the dominant manufacturer, Apple, has insisted on charging high fees and controlling economically valuable information about customers. Each new device brings an additional level of complexity and expense. Not long ago, "convergence" was the keyword in news production, as television, newspaper, magazine and pure online sites all started to look the same. Now comes a new "divergence," in which online journalism organizations must distribute news into distinctly different modes of presentation.

The iPad has been a hit: Expectations are that about 30 million devices will have shipped by the end of 2011.[1] But while analysts expect the iPad to capture more than 90 percent of the tablet market in 2011, competitors are entering the fray. Tablet manufacturers have announced that more than 25 brands will be available in 2011, at screen sizes ranging from five to 11 inches.[2]

Audiences are fragmenting in other ways, too—in their interests and habits. The conflict is evident in the behavior of Michael Harwayne, vice president of digital strategy and development at Time Inc. Harwayne lives in Manhattan and takes the subway to work. He likes to read the Wall Street Journal on his commute, but lately the question has been: Which format works best?

Harwayne likes the Amazon Kindle. When the Journal became available on that device in the spring of 2009, he decided to pay an extra $10 per month for the convenience, though he was already paying $363 per year for the print and web editions. The Kindle price rose to $15 per month a year later.

But there was no connection between his print/online subscription and the Kindle edition, and Harwayne found it annoying to be billed separately. Then, in May 2010, came the Wall Street Journal iPad app, which he got as part of his overall subscription. It's not that it was "free," but because he didn't have to pay a separate fee, it felt free. Still, he said, "I didn't like carrying it and reading it on the subway, so I never actually canceled the Kindle until I had a lightweight alternative."

In the fall of 2010, he was introduced to a Samsung tablet. He liked it more than the iPad, so he switched to the Journal's Android version (which is also included in his core subscription to the paper) and finally canceled his Kindle subscription. But Harwayne wondered, "Why shouldn't I be able to read the paper on any device I have?"

In March 2011, he learned that he'll eventually have to pay an additional $17.29 a month to keep his iPad or Android version of the Wall Street Journal. Through it all, the one thing that hasn't changed is that Harwayne likes to read the print version of the Journal after a long day at work. Still, it "seems like a very strange consumer strategy," he says.

Early data about tablets appeared to show great promise for news organizations. A few months after the first iPad went on the market in the spring of 2010, the Associated Press reported that Gannett Co. was getting $50 per thousand page views for iPad advertisements—or five times the price it was getting on its websites.[3] Condé Nast initially said visitors were spending an hour with each of its iPad issues—far more than the three or four minutes per visit its websites draw and close to the overall print magazine average of 70 minutes.[4] David Carey, president of Hearst Magazines, said in March 2011 that the company would end the year with "several hundred thousand subscriptions in total" sold through digital publisher Zinio, Barnes & Noble's Nook e-reader and Apple's iPad. He predicted that as much as 25 percent of his company's subscribers will be on tablets "in the next five years."[5]

But making predictions based on early and volatile sales is tricky. The data on usage of tablets and smartphones come from products—and a competitive environment—that are in transition. Many buyers are early adapters to technology, a group whose behavior does not reliably predict the greater population who will eventually buy the gadgets. (Of the 66 million smartphone users in the U.S., only about a third have used the browser or downloaded an app, according to audience measurement company comScore.[6])

Wired, a magazine with a tech-savvy readership, sold 100,000 single copies via the iPad in June 2010, but that number dropped to 22,000 by October; in 2011, its single-copy iPad sales have averaged 20,000 to 30,000 per issue.[7] Wired's average monthly circulation of 800,000 still consists mostly of print subscriptions and single-copy sales; a small number (27,000) are sold as PDF-based digital replicas.[8] It's likely that the high price and one-issue limit of Wired's iPad version have hindered sales; one copy costs $4.99—the same as a copy sold at the newsstand—while an annual print subscription starts at around $12 a year. And the froth has settled throughout the company: In April 2011, a Condé Nast publisher told AdAge that the company's iPad strategy was slowing: "They're not all doing all that well, so why rush to get them all on there?"[9]

One issue is Apple's own pricing strategy. The company announced in early 2011 that it wants a 30 percent cut of any subscriptions paid through the iTunes store.[10] More important, when the user pays with a credit card stored in iTunes—

and Apple had about 200 million registered users in 2011[11]—the user's name and address don't have to be shared with the publisher, unless the customer agrees. Without this information, publishers have a handicap: They can't find out the particulars of their subscribers' reading behavior. Google is pushing an alternative tool for subscriptions called One Pass, in which the company will charge publishers 10 percent of revenue and share subscribers' names and information. Some publishers, such as Time Inc., have built their own payment and collection systems for selling their own apps from their own websites so they don't have to share any information or pay any fees.[12]

For most magazines, neither the replica digital copies nor the iPad versions of their magazines count in the "rate base," which is the number of readers publishers guarantee to deliver to advertisers. So, for now, publishers tout it as "bonus" circulation they can't really charge for.

Some news organizations are optimistic about the economics of mobile devices. In March 2011, Dow Jones announced that it had 200,000 paying subscribers who access to the Wall Street Journal via some sort of mobile device.[13] The company did not say how much additional revenue this brought in, so many of these readers could be like Michael Harwayne—digital subscribers who signed up for mobile access. (The Wall Street Journal's total reported average daily paid circulation is about 2 million copies—1.6 million copies in print and 430,000 electronic copies.[14])

Time Inc. announced plans in February 2011 to give Time, Fortune, People and Sports Illustrated subscribers the ability to access those magazines' content on multiple platforms.[15] Sports Illustrated has been particularly aggressive in digital expansion; to introduce its digital package as widely as possible, it has given access to all 3.15 million of its current print subscribers. For new customers, it is promoting an "All Access" subscription plan, which includes the print magazine, plus access via tablet, web and smartphone; in March 2011, the price for All Access (including a bonus windbreaker) was $48 per year.[16] A digital-only package with no magazine and no jacket costs the same. That pricing scheme helps protect the print edition and provides the biggest possible digital audience.

Some publishers are willing to invest a lot to gamble on an unknown future and avoid sitting on the sidelines.

In February 2011, News Corp. launched The Daily, a tablet-only newspaper. First offered on just the iPad, though there are plans to extend it to more tablets, The Daily announced a start-up budget of $30 million, which let it hire enough journalists, designers and technicians to create 100 pages of content per day. Integrated into the Daily are features that seem to shine on the iPad platform, such as social-media links, audio and video. Greg Clayman, publisher of the Daily, said hundreds of thousands of users have downloaded the app, but he's not ready to reveal how many use it on a regular basis.[17]

George Rodrigue, managing editor of the Dallas Morning News, says the iPad "may be the thing that helps people read enterprise journalism. We used to say you have to be platform agnostic. I don't think that's right anymore. You have to be platform specific." But the transition isn't cheap. "We have to build a staff for the iPad—two people plus an assignment editor," he says. "We're going to handcraft little stories summarizing every story—55 words max. Every reporter will write the summary themselves. Every section front will be a summary of the news page." At the Miami Herald, Raul Lopez, the interactive general manager, estimates the paper's total digital page views to be 30 million per month; about 2 million are mobile, and half of those are via the iPhone.

* * *

Meanwhile, video has become an essential element of the digital experience. According to comScore, about 89 million people in the U.S. watched at least one online video, or video advertisement, daily by the end of 2010.[18]

For journalism sites, broadband access has made video distribution more feasible. But persuading users to watch news video isn't easy. Online video journalism is becoming a world of haves and have-nots. Among the haves, CNN.com reigns supreme.

"In any given month, well over half our unique visitors watch video," says K.C. Estenson, senior vice president and general manager of CNN.com. "The percentage has gone up every year." When CNN.com redesigned its site in 2009, the network "anchored it on video," Estenson says. It isn't unusual for the website to have 15 or more video links on its home page, including at least three or four in high-profile featured positions.

CNN.com is different than other video-rich sites because of the size and expectations of its audience. The company says it delivers between 60 million and 100 million video streams a month. In contrast to local-broadcast competitors, CNN.com can match the costs of substantial technology and newsgathering with a massive audience. "If you do not have scale, you do not have a business," says Estenson. CNN.com has also launched a free iPad application in which video is integrated into text. And CNN is hungry for more viewers. Estenson says CNN can sell "almost every single video impression we create. So we would like more video consumption."

CNN has brought its broadcast expertise onto the Web. "We program by times of day," says Estenson. "The bell curve of visitors to our site peaks between 11 a.m. and 2 p.m. on regular news days. We've noticed that social media links go up a lot at night." Sometimes CNN makes programming decisions based on a mix of demographic and editorial priorities. Estenson notes that users under the age of 25, who "are disproportionately on social media," tend to be more interested in entertainment and features rather than in hard news. So, while "CNN is all about trust and reliability," Estenson says, "for CNN.com, entertainment is one of the biggest sections of the site."

Estenson sees contrasts between the content on CNN's cable channel and CNN.com. Online, producers have more freedom to experiment and expand, and the content can be more daring. "Going online is a private experience, versus watching in the living room. When people are online, they seem to gravitate to things that are more provocative than they would if they were in a room with their friends."

How profitable is CNN online? According to a presentation the network made to analysts in mid-2010, revenue for CNN overall (consisting of the U.S. and international divisions, Headline News and digital) was about $500 million; digital advertising and content sales accounted for about 10 percent of total revenue.[19] CNN.com's profit margin isn't broken out publicly by either its division, Turner Broadcasting System Inc., or by the parent company, Time Warner Inc. Estenson does say the digital operations have been profitable for the last seven years—even including corporate costs and just under 100 "dedicated digital" people on the editorial side. All of CNN benefits from a centralized publishing platform; sales and administrative expenses are spread across the three television divisions and their online properties.

CNN.com is dependent mostly on ad revenue that is sold directly by a CNN sales force. But the digital business also gets some direct corporate support. Estenson says a "select portion" of the subscription money that cable and satellite companies pay to carry CNN's programming is used for research and development activities related to new technologies, such as smartphones, tablets and televisions connected to the Web. Thus, benefits from CNN's digital investments flow both ways, from the traditional to the digital and back.

Estenson believes the site feeds viewers and value back to the legacy network. "Digital platforms are the entry point for the brand. More and more people will discover the brand through them," he says. And he envisions some of the distinctions between the two platforms becoming less relevant, especially as the Internet gets a bigger foothold in living rooms.

CNN.com is something of an exception in its success with online video. Most local TV stations' websites have far less traffic and revenue. In interviews with executives at a station based in one of the top five metropolitan areas of the country, a more difficult picture emerges. (The station was willing to share metrics on the condition it not be identified.) In October 2010, the station's website attracted about 7 million page views. But it delivered only 622,000 video streams that month. The station's general manager said that when video became feasible on the Web several years ago, executives believed they would have a natural competitive advantage. "We thought having video was the key to becoming a popular website. But only 10 percent of the visitors look at video." And partly as a result of the low video usage online, only 1 percent of the station's total advertising revenue comes from its website.

The general manager has seen statistics that show similarly paltry results at other local television stations' sites. One problem, he says, is that other sites are also producing video, so broadcast stations face more competition for views. Sports fans appear to be particularly interested in newspaper sites' video.[20] He has thought about doing more consumer research but can't justify the expense. "No one is buying the site, really," he says, "so it's not worth spending more money to figure it out."

Somewhere between this station's frustration and CNN.com's success is LIN Media, a company that owns 32 local television stations in markets ranging from Springfield, Mass., to Albuquerque, N.M. LIN delivered 116 million video streams in 2010, and has built its business on shared operations and costs, as well as long-term investment in branding and marketing.[21]

LIN is in 17 markets, and the company has multiple stations in several cities. It is in small or medium-sized "DMAs"—that is, "designated market areas" that are defined and ranked by Nielsen, the audience-rating company. The markets range from Indianapolis (25th largest in the country) to Providence, R.I., (53rd) to Lafayette, Ind. (191st).[22] LIN controls costs by having one building, one staff, and one newsroom per market, with costs shared by all its stations in that market. For non-local topics such as health, LIN produces stories that serve all of its markets. Companywide, LIN has about 200 digital employees in a workforce of 2,000. (Four years ago, it had nine digital employees in a workforce of 2,300.) Robb Richter, LIN's senior vice president for new media, says the video the company produces for broadcast is its competitive advantage. "We have mounds of video we can use"—something most other sites lack.

Print-based media are still building video resources and expertise. Even those with successful sites have had a hard time winning a video audience. Michael Silberman, general manager of New York Magazine's popular site, says nymag.com has tried to integrate video into its editorial content but that the pace of video and the commitment to watch it still aren't working for most visitors. The site features videos it produces in-house as well as material from around the Web that is "curated" by online editors, based on subject matter, relevance and news value. So, for example, nymag.com has a food video page with categories beyond news, such as restaurants, chefs and recipes. But it's hard to build an audience, Silberman says, adding, "If your site isn't about video, people don't click on it." For nymag.com, less than 10 percent of unique users go to video. At Huffington Post, no more than 5 percent of unique visitors clicked on a video throughout most of 2010.[23]

Lewis DVorkin, chief product officer of Forbes Media, agrees. "Video on the web is hard. It's very stressful," he says. Since joining Forbes in the spring of 2010, DVorkin has been coming up with new ways to create and distribute Forbes content. But video has him stumped: "We had a difficult video strategy. It was conceived on the broadcast model—produced, highly expensive, and it involved lots of people." He foresees moving to outside contributors more in video, as he has done elsewhere on Forbes.com. DVorkin and nymag's Silberman both say that until they unlock the video puzzle, they are losing opportunities for ad revenue. Silberman says, "Our ad demand outstrips our audience demand."

The Wall Street Journal's site has drawn significant traffic and revenue to its video offerings. The site serves around 8 million streams a month, says Alan Murray, deputy managing editor and executive editor, online, for the Journal. And the ad rates are healthy—$30 to $40 per thousand views (or CPMs). The site features live videos before and after the market closes, and they're often displayed prominently on the home page. Unlike much of the rest of the site, viewing the videos doesn't require a subscription.

The key to making video profitable, Murray says, is controlling costs. WSJ.com has about 16 people devoted to video production, and the company has trained many of its print reporters in basic video techniques. "If you go to Bahrain and need a satellite truck, that's $25,000," Murray says. "All we need is a $200 iPhone 4." WSJ.com has also managed to get viewers to watch video during work hours, something that many other sites have found difficult.

The Miami Herald recently noted that its video traffic grew by 25 percent in 2010.[24] Videos that the Herald produces and hosts on its site get about 200,000 streams a month, says Lopez, the interactive general manager. That is a relatively small number, given that the site gets more than 6 million visitors per month.

The Herald has bolstered its video presence with segments produced by the Associated Press and other organizations. It also tried to distinguish itself by producing longer videos of newsmakers talking about various topics, but those are a tough sell online. "There's a reason that television does two-minute stories," the Herald's managing editor, Rick Hirsch, told Poynter.org. "Unless something is super compelling, people's attention span is relatively short, and it's even shorter on a small screen." And it's not easy to make the advertising numbers work. Lopez says Herald-produced videos earn just $4,000 per month—that is, 200,000 streams a month at $20 per thousand viewers.

Cynthia Carr, senior vice president of sales at the Dallas Morning News, also doubts video will become a significant profit driver any time soon. "We're not monetizing video. I don't see that bringing big revenue," she says. Dallasnews.com got an average of 186,000 video streams a month in 2010, clicked on by 2 percent of the unique visitors coming to the site.

And video traffic is hard to anticipate. Like Hollywood, there are hits and flops—as the Detroit Free Press found in January 2011, when it ran a dramatic video of a shootout in a local police station.[25] It got nearly 714,000 streams, or nearly half the total traffic to video on Detroit's site for a three-month period. When it launched, the video was preceded by a short commercial. But within seven hours and 70,000 streams, a reader who went by the name "HartlandRunner" posted this comment: "I am glad you are willing to tell this story by showing the video, but why the ad beforehand? Brutality brought to us by UnitedHealth Care? ...Very, very tacky, even in an online world. ... This tape was paid for by taxpayers and shows graphic real violence ... and you guys put an ad on it. That's unbelievable and I hope you change it."

Nancy Andrews, Detroit Free Press's managing editor for digital media, said, "I saw the comment and checked with the vice president of advertising. She said let's take the ad off." So they removed the ad, and forfeited some revenue—but kept readers happy. And it did help editors understand even more about how news video works on the Internet. "People are interested in the raw video content," Andrews says. "Show me what happened. ... You don't necessarily need the context in video form, too. ... Think of it more like a picture that talks than a full story."

---

[1] Bryan Chaffin, "Analyst Ups Q4 iPad Shipments to 6.3 Million," The Mac Observer, Dec. 2, 2010. http://bit.ly/fVdrQD; Yenting Chen and Joseph Tsai, "Apple expects shipments of 6-6.5 million iPads in 1Q11," Digitimes, March 2, 2011, http://bit.ly/fEiSkb; Pascal-Emmanuel

Gobry, "iPad Shipments Will Hit 65 Million In 2011, Says Analyst," Business Insider, Dec. 29, 2010. http://read.bi/hDFy5C; Anna Johnson, "iPad Sales To Grow By 127 Percent in 2011," Kikabink News, Dec. 15, 2010. http://bit.ly/fQXWNy

2 Mobile DTV and ITV presentation by Pearl consortium at Borrell conference, March 3, 2011.

3 Andrew Vanacore, "Publishers see signs the iPad can restore ad money," Associated Press, June 3, 2010, http://usat.ly/f9wnqi.

4 Joe Pompeo, "iPad Owners Spend An Hour Or More Reading A Single Magazine On The Device," Business Insider, June 7, 2010. http://read.bi/htam4c

5 Christopher Hosford, "Tablets, contextual ads drive discussion at summit," B2B, March 14, 2011. http://bit.ly/eNlYji; David Kaplan, "Hearst's Carey: Tablets Will Provide 25 Percent Of Magazines' Circulation" paidcontent.org, March 9, 2011. http://bit.ly/ibBilx

6 "comScore Reports January 2011 U.S. Mobile Subscriber Market Share," comScore, March 7, 2011. http://bit.ly/gPjCfz

7 John Koblin, "Memo Pad: iPad Magazine Sales Drop," WWDMedia, Dec. 29, 2010. http://bit.ly/gSJg66 Also see Peter Kafka, "Wired's Newest iPad Issue Boasts Its Best Feature Yet: Free" AllThingsDigital, April 15, 2011. http://bit.ly/dImJ8w

8 ABC Publisher's Statement, Dec. 31, 2010.

9 Nat Ives, "Conde Nast Taps Brakes on Churning Out iPad Editions for All Its Magazines," AdAge, April 22, 2011, http://bit.ly/i6KHv7.

10 Existing customers who subscribe to an app from a publisher's website and use the publisher's billing services aren't subject to the fee.

11 MG Siegler, "Apple Now Has 200 Million iTunes Accounts, Biggest Credit Card Hub On Web" TechCrunch, March 2, 2011. http://tcrn.ch/fRLtFW

12 Amir Efrati, Mary Lane and Russell Adams, "Google Elbows Apple, Woos Publishers," Wall Street Journal, Feb. 17, 2011. http://on.wsj.com/iaYu7B

13 Aparajita Saha-Bubna, "The Journal Adds 200,000 Mobile-Device Subscribers," Wall Street Journal, March 11, 2011. http://on.wsj.com/gzVUZZ

14 ABC Audit Statement, September 30, 2010

15 John Biggs, "Time Inc. Releases Sports Illustrated Digital Subscriptions," TechCrunch, Feb. 11, 2011. http://tcrn.ch/fG5mW4

16 In March 2011, Sports Illustrated subscriptions were priced in various ways. An "All Access" subscription was billed at $4.99 monthly and included an Android app, print magazine and web access. The same plan paid by the year cost $48 and included a free windbreaker. A digital-only subscription costs $3.99 a month.

17 Staci Kramer, "'Daily' Publisher Disputes Subscription Numbers; Says 5,000 Far Too Low," paidcontent.org, March 17, 2011. http://bit.ly/eeqQ2A

18 "The comScore 2010 U.S. Digital Year in Review," comScore, Feb. 7, 2011, page 22. http://bit.ly/eq7mjE

[19] Alex Weprin, "This Is Where CNN Makes Its Money," TVNewser, May 27, 2010. http://bit.ly/edQDUd

[20] Borrell Associates, "Benchmarking Local Online Media: 2010 Revenue Survey," March 2011. http://bit.ly/eSBkXU

[21] News Release. "LIN TV Corp. Announces Fourth Quarter and Full Year 2010 Results," March 16, 2011. http://bit.ly/gvSTwP

[22] LIN Media website: http://bit.ly/hGC6Up

[23] Based on internal count of unique users in 2010.

[24] Mallary Jean Tenore, "How The Miami Herald cultivates loyal audience for video, its second biggest traffic driver," Poynter.org, Feb. 2, 2011. http://bit.ly/dSPxQT

[25] "Watch video released by Detroit police showing police station gun battle," Detroit Free Press, Jan. 28, 2011, http://bit.ly/eYVfiQ.

Chapter 5

Paywalls: *Information at a Price*

"Information wants to be free. Information also wants to be expensive. In-formation wants to be free because it has become so cheap to distribute, copy, and recombine—too cheap to meter. It wants to be expensive because it can be immeasurably valuable to the recipient. That tension will not go away. ... Each round of new devices makes the tension worse, not better."
—Stewart Brand, *The Media Lab*, 1987[1]

"The Internet is the most effective means of giving stuff away for free that humanity has ever devised. Actually making money from it is not just hard, it may be fundamentally opposed to the character and momentum of the net."
—John Lanchester, London Review of Books essay, 2010[2]

When the Wall Street Journal decided to charge for its online edition in 1996, the company did so without a great deal of deliberation. Rather, as Peter Kann, who was then the chief executive officer of the Journal's parent company, Dow Jones, would later recall, "I didn't know any better. I just thought people should pay for content."[3]

That was a novel idea at the time—that people should pay for news they got on the Web. Today, after years of declining print circulation and disappointing online ad revenue, many news organizations have begun pondering whether to institute a subscription system for their online sites.

Pondering is still all most companies have done, though increasingly they are warming to the idea of charging for at least some of their digital content. Their hesitation stems from several concerns. Some are fearful they will lose so much Web traffic that their online advertising revenue will fall significantly; others are daunted by the technological hurdles involved in getting a new online subscriber system to work in tandem with the one that has served print customers for years.

Also, subscription revenue has historically been such a small factor in the ad-driven media business that many news organizations wonder if they would ever get much return on the investment.

Publishers usually cite three reasons to charge for online products. One, of course, is to increase subscription revenue. Another, less obvious, is to stanch the erosion in legacy operations: That is, since their readers now get the content they want for free online, why would they pay for a print subscription? If you start charging for digital access, shouldn't that protect your more profitable print business? Finally, there is evidence that a paying audience is more valuable to advertisers because it demonstrates deeper commitment by those readers.

A few online-only news organizations have tried pay schemes, usually to charge for premium content beyond their free websites. Politico launched its "Pro" version in early 2011, charging $2,495 a year for in-depth coverage of such topics as energy or health care.[4] That puts Politico into competition with older publications like Congressional Quarterly, now owned by the Economist Group, and newcomers like Bloomberg Government. At a much lower price, ESPN.com offers access to its "Insider" site, with exclusive blogs, videos and tools, at prices ranging from $30 to more than $70 a year. And to ensure there's a bundle, online subscribers also get ESPN The Magazine, a biweekly print publication.

The paywall issue is especially acute for newspaper sites. In the months leading up to publication of this report, most of the attention of journalists was directed at the New York Times' new digital subscription service. Before that, though, the conversation about paywalls in the U.S. has focused on two staunch believers in the digital subscription business: the Wall Street Journal, which began charging in 1996 shortly after its website launched, and the Arkansas Democrat-Gazette, which started imposing online subscriptions in 2002.

Walter Hussman, publisher of the Arkansas paper, has portrayed his site's paywall as a way to protect the more lucrative print edition. The online subscription service "does not justify itself as a revenue stream," Hussman has said.[5] Print subscribers get the online edition for free.

The Wall Street Journal sees it differently and has consistently charged print subscribers extra for digital access. And the difference between those strategies is manifested in the publications' number of digital subscribers: WSJ.com has around 1.1 million subscribers (including those who also get the print edition), or a bit more than half of its print base. The Democrat-Gazette has around 4,400 subscribers to its "electronic edition"—about 2 percent of its daily circulation base. Its print circulation, though, has remained remarkably steady while that of other papers has declined precipitously. In 2006, the Democrat-Gazette's daily circulation was 176,910. Daily circulation now is listed at 186,962, though some of that strength is due to a merger of operations with some small Arkansas papers whose subscribers are now counted in the Democrat-Gazette's total.[6]

But how replicable are these two models? The Wall Street Journal provides content geared toward financial decision making and reaches a more elite and affluent audience than most news organizations. The Arkansas paper is the dominant news organization in its state.

To see how news executives figure out whether to charge online, we examined the decision-making processes at two large metro newspapers—the Dallas Morning News and the Miami Herald. Each thought about the same issues, relied on similar data—and then embarked upon completely different strategies.

Both papers have histories as journalistic powerhouses in their home markets. The Herald, which has been owned by McClatchy since 2006, has won 20 Pulitzer Prizes, on subjects ranging from local election fraud to the Iran-Contra scandal. The Morning News has won nine Pulitzers and has dominated the Dallas market since its parent company, Belo, bought and closed the rival Times Herald in 1991.

But both have experienced significant declines in their print circulation, and both had reason to believe that their free websites might be partly to blame.

At the Herald, circulation had been steadily declining for years. The Herald and its Spanish-language sibling, El Nuevo Herald, fell from a combined daily circulation of 393,382 in 2005 to 261,657 in 2009. Most of the decline was outside the Herald's "city zone"—its core in Miami-Dade County. The Herald has also cut back discounted bulk circulation to schools, hotels and other institutions.[7]

The trend has been similar in Dallas, where the Morning News has dropped from 373,586 daily circulation in 2007 to 264,459 in 2010. In part, that is also because the paper began to focus on its most loyal print subscribers a few years ago. The News trimmed back most of its delivery beyond a 100-mile radius of Dallas, though it still circulates in Austin, the state capital, which is 200 miles away. "We reduced footprint in the state," says John Walsh, senior vice president for circulation at the Morning News. "Advertisers were saying they're not interested outside the core market." That helped eliminate some extraneous expenses. It took so long to get newspapers to Odessa, about 350 miles west of Dallas, that the delivery person "had to spend the night in a motel after delivering the paper," Walsh says. "It was like the Pony Express." The Morning News also eliminated much of its single-copy sales effort, removing 9,000 of its 10,000 newspaper racks around the metro area.

A few years ago, the News began doing studies about the price sensitivity of its subscribers. Executives wanted to know if the remaining readers were now a core of the faithful who would be willing to pay much higher prices for home delivery. One study indicated that a 40 percent hike in the price of a subscription would result in a loss of around 12 percent of its subscribers, says Publisher James Moroney. That emboldened executives to raise the price of a monthly subscription aggressively, from $21 to $30 in May 2009 and then to $33.95 in 2011—one of the highest prices for any metropolitan paper in the country.

In those days, Moroney was convinced that free digital access was the way to go. In May 2009, he told a U.S. Senate committee holding hearings on the state of the newspaper business that "if The Dallas Morning News today put up a paywall over its content, people would go to the Fort Worth Star-Telegram."[8]

Within a few months, though, Moroney began reconsidering his aversion to a paywall. In remarks in the fall of 2010 to a small group at the Carnegie Corporation, Moroney provided this analysis: "The Morning News does 40 million page views a month. If we could sell out three ad positions on every page every day at a $7 CPM, we would yield $10 million" a year.[9] That, he noted, would cover less than a third of his editorial costs—even as those costs have dropped as newsroom staffing has fallen from 660 at its peak to around 400.

More fundamentally, Moroney had concluded that a focus on volume—either in the form of cheap print subscriptions or of Web traffic that generated insufficient revenue—had damaged the news industry's economic vitality. "What I most fear about this obsession with volume is it underlies the persistent belief that if we will just grow sufficiently large audiences online, then eventually we will sell enough advertising to be sustainably profitable," he told the group. He added, "There is more supply [of online ads] than there is demand. And the explosive growth of social media only ensures this imbalance of supply and demand will persist for a considerable period of time."

Others at the Morning News noticed that traffic to the Web site had grown as print subscription rates rose. Why pay more for print, some readers seem to have reasoned, when you can get the same news free online? "We found when we raised the price of the paper, a lot of people migrated to dallasnews.com," says Executive Editor Bob Mong.

The News launched an aggressive pricing scheme for its digital content in February 2011. People who don't subscribe to the paper must pay $16.95 a month to get access to the Web, iPad and iPhone versions of the Morning News. Print subscribers already paying $33.95 a month get unlimited access to any digital edition.

It is a paywall, but not an absolute one. Stories that strike the editors as "commodity" journalism—such as breaking news, or weather and traffic updates that could easily be found elsewhere—are free to all. More proprietary or exclusive journalism requires a subscription. (Currently, about half of the stories on the site's home page have open access.)

When Moroney announced the pay plan, he and his staff were predicting that page views would drop by 40 to 50 percent. "I'm not confident we're going to succeed," he told Nieman Journalism Lab. "But we've got to try something."[10] In an interview a few weeks before the paywall launched, he portrayed the strategy as a way to help return journalism to one of its former, and highly profitable, roles as a one-stop storehouse of local news. "At least for a period of time, you can restore the bundle," he said.

In late April 2011, six weeks after the pay plan launched, the News did see traffic declines—though less, so far, than Moroney had predicted. Unique visitors were down 17 percent, and page views declined 28 percent, compared to the same period in 2010. Mark Medici, director of audience development for the News, declined to disclose how many new digital subscribers had signed up, but did say that 27 percent of print subscribers had enrolled for digital access.

Traffic declines were also on the minds of Miami Herald executives when they debated whether to institute a pay plan.

The Herald did a survey on its site in October 2009 to determine users' willingness to pay for its content. It was a voluntary and thus unscientific poll; nevertheless, the results didn't inspire a great deal of confidence. Fifteen percent said they'd pay for unlimited access; an additional 23 percent said "maybe." The dollar amounts weren't meaningful, though; less than 5 percent said they would spend more than $10 a month.

Another survey question asked readers if they would make a "voluntary financial payment" to support the Herald's site. Nearly a third said they were very or somewhat likely to do so, and so a few weeks later, the Herald's site instituted a "tip jar," attaching this plea to many pages on the site: "If you value The Miami Herald's local news reporting and investigations, but prefer the convenience of the Internet, please consider a voluntary payment for the Web news that matters to you." Says Armando Boniche, the Herald's circulation director: "We got about $1,000 to $2,000 total. McClatchy [the Herald's parent company] had us pull it after six weeks."

Meanwhile, the Herald increased print subscription prices, though not to the extent that Dallas did, and stopped discounting the paper in Broward County, just north of its home market. And the Herald made a few smaller price-enhancing moves, such as charging 50 cents a week for an insert with TV listings and $1 extra for the ad-filled Thanksgiving Day newspaper. (Still, old habits die hard. In January 2011, the Herald was offering six months of seven-day delivery for just 77 cents a week—a whopping 83 percent discount from its stated price.)

The Herald also did some paywall calculations, modifying formulas provided by the Newspaper Association of America. In 2009, when the study was prepared, Miamiherald.com was attracting around 3.88 million unique visitors and 25.2 million page views a month. Its advertising mix was typical of many news organizations of its size. The Herald's own ad department sold 42 percent of the total space available on the site, at prices averaging slightly over $13 per 1,000 views. An additional 36 percent of the available advertising space on the site was sold as "remnant"—very cheap—ads, under $1 CPMs. And 22 percent of the ad inventory on the site went unsold altogether.

The Herald first modeled what would happen if it imposed what Boniche calls a "10-foot wall" that would require a 99-cent monthly subscription for anyone to read anything on the site. The company predicted page views would fall by 91 percent, and total revenue from the site would drop by 76 percent. In other words, new subscription revenue wouldn't come close to compensating for the ad dollars that would vanish as the audience contracted.

Herald executives mapped out several scenarios in which they could institute a paywall and match the results they were getting with a free site whose income was entirely from advertising. But all of the ideas required substantial leaps of faith.

One scenario, charging just 99 cents a month for digital access, would require the Herald to attract 335,000 subscribers—about 30 percent more than the combined daily print circulation of the English- and Spanish-language newspapers. Another option: The Herald could make do with only 50,000 digital subscribers, but it would have to charge them nearly $120 a year—almost as much as a Wall Street Journal online subscription. Or, the site could enroll 50,000 subscribers at a more reasonable price (99 cents a month), but the paper would have to get advertisers to pay an impossible six to ten times its current rates for online ads.

Given how remote any of those possibilities seemed, the Herald analysis suggested that the most sensible approach to a paywall would be a hybrid model with 1 percent of users—about 38,000—paying $1.99 a month for unlimited access, and nonsubscribers getting a great deal of access as well. That would preserve the site's traffic and advertising. But the revenue boost from digital subscriptions would be less than $1 million a year, and that sum, which represents less than 1 percent of the company's overall revenue, didn't seem worth the investment in time, marketing and other costs.

*   *   *

One publisher whose digital subscription base has grown substantially is the Financial Times.

The FT started charging for access in 2001 and had a modest number of online subscribers for many years, getting to 126,000 online subscribers in 2009, slightly less than a third of its print subscription base.[11] Subscriptions leapt to 207,000 in 2010, or more than half the number of print subscribers. And digital access isn't cheap—the FT charges $259 a year for a standard subscription and $389 for premium access to more content deep within the site.[12]

The growth is tied to a change in strategy. Nonsubscribers used to be able to come to FT.com and read 10 free stories without registering; after registering, they could get 30 more stories a month before the subscription requirement kicked in. (This is similar to the "metered" approach that was put into effect in 2011 by the New York Times.) The FT toughened its policy in 2007 by preventing nonsubscribers from getting any stories without registration and limiting them to 10 stories a month before the paywall rises.

So, the wall has become less permeable. But Rob Grimshaw, managing director of FT.com, says there is a more fundamental change at work: Managers "used to approach it as newspaper marketing;" now they realize they "are direct Internet retailers."

That means using behavioral targeting to determine which of the nearly 3 million nonpaying, registered users are most likely to subscribe and directing appeals to them. "What topics are people reading? We developed a dynamic model to determine readers' propensity to subscribe"—one that is constantly shifting, with changes being made "on a daily basis," Grimshaw says. "We're spending the same amount on marketing as we used to, but we more than doubled our rate of acquisition."

The FT has also been aggressive about shutting down "leakage," as Grimshaw puts it—that is, unauthorized copying of stories. And when it comes to offering free content, "we're more controlled than WSJ.com," which offers free access to most of its stories via Google News and many stories at no charge on its home page.

The FT's approach is a testament to the possibilities of paid content, but it also demonstrates how hard it is even for a premium publisher to extract revenue from digital advertising. When the FT's parent company, Pearson, reported results in early 2011, it noted that for the FT Group, 55 percent of its revenue comes from "content/subscriptions" while 45 percent comes from advertising.[13] A decade ago, the FT earned 74 percent of its revenue from ads, and only 26 percent from subscriptions.

"The outlook for the ad business online is quite bleak," says Grimshaw. "There's just not enough money there." As a subscription site with a select audience, FT.com can charge higher rates for ads than general-interest sites. "We can create scarcity in a marketplace that has no scarcity," he says. "In that light, subscriptions and ads are complementary." But given that FT.com doesn't use networks to fill up unsold ad space at discount prices, Grimshaw says "I'd be surprised if we sell 50 percent" of the site's inventory.

*　*　*

After years of internal debate, the New York Times has entered the realm of pay-for-access. If its audacious and complex plan succeeds, that will likely encourage many other publishers to follow suit.

This isn't the first time the company has tried online subscriptions. In 2005, the Times launched its TimesSelect service, charging those who didn't get the print edition $49 a year to access opinion pieces. After a fast start, with more than 120,000 subscribers signing up in two months, the plan stalled, and the Times closed it down two years later; executives said the $10 million a year the service was generating wasn't enough to compensate for the lost traffic and ad revenue.[14]

So why would the Times take a new gamble to charge for digital access? Part of the answer lies in how dramatically the company's revenue mix has changed in recent years.

In 2005, the New York Times Media Group, which is composed primarily of the Times' paper and website, generated nearly $1.9 billion in ad and subscription revenue; about a third of that came from circulation. Five years later, ad revenue had dropped by nearly $500 million, while circulation revenue had increased because of aggressive price hikes for home delivery and newsstand sales. Today, circulation revenue for the group almost equals advertising revenue.

New York Times Media Group revenue mix

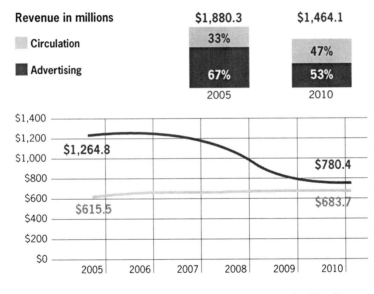

The New York Times Media Group includes the Times and the International Herald Tribune, print and digital, as well as a few smaller properties. Results are not broken out in more detail by the company.

SOURCE: Based on the New York Times Co. 10-K filings

The Times' website is tremendously popular, but digital ads have been growing unevenly and don't come close to making up for the shortfall in print ad sales. Indeed, the site, with more than 30 million monthly unique users in the U.S., contributes less than 20 percent of the Times' overall revenue.

So the Times devised a pay scheme that it hoped would be porous enough to allow occasional readers (around 85 percent of the total) to browse the site for free, but priced aggressively enough to generate significant revenue from its most devoted readers.[15] It was a difficult plan to execute—requiring more than 14 months, and reportedly costing tens of millions of dollars.[16]

When the Times introduced the plan in March 2011, many found it to be unnecessarily complex. Users are supposed to be limited to 20 stories a month before they hit the wall. But because there are so many exceptions depending on how one accesses the site—for example, via Google, Twitter or a blog—even some experts are befuddled by the plan. Staci Kramer, editor of paidcontent.org, which covers the digital media industry, wrote that "the logistics are far more complex than anything should be that doesn't require a degree in quantum physics."[17] There are different rates for online, smartphone and tablet access, ranging from $195 to $455 a year for the full package. Consumers can't get annual, or even monthly, subscriptions, because everything is priced in four-week increments. And the price led one commentator to headline his blog post, "The New York Times is Delusional."[18]

The Times is unusual among big publishers in that it doesn't require print subscribers to pay anything to access its digital editions. Both WSJ.com and FT.com have long charged everyone for online access, on the theory that digital editions offer utility, archives and tools that the print edition can't. The Times is offering its print readers a sweet deal: Weekend-only subscribers can pay as little as $327 a year, and in the bargain get a digital package worth almost a third more. Times executives insist this isn't an effort to prop up the company's more lucrative legacy revenue. "We didn't make this decision to bolster print," Janet Robinson, the Times' company CEO, said shortly after the pay plan debuted. "We made this decision to create a new revenue stream."[19] But given the way the offer is structured, it's hard to argue that the two aren't closely tied. The pricing—which is higher for tablets than for the Web—also reflects Apple's decision to take a 30 percent cut of subscriptions purchased through iTunes.

A few weeks after the Times instituted the pay plan, Robinson reported that more than 100,000 people had signed up for digital subscriptions.[20] Most of those were enrolled for the introductory offer of 99 cents for the first four weeks, according to a person close to the situation, so it isn't clear how that will play out when those subscribers start getting billed up to $35 for every four weeks of unlimited access.

In the Times' own story on its plan, a senior editor called the plan "essentially a bet that you can reconstitute to some degree the print economics online."[21] In fact, though, it is as much an effort to restore print economics to the print edition, by providing extra value to subscribers and giving them one less reason to forgo the lucrative newspaper for the digital edition.

*   *   *

And then there is the Newport Daily News, a 12,000-circulation newspaper in Rhode Island.

In 2009, the News decided that it was almost impossible to make money from digital ads. "The people we hired to sell advertising on the Internet just never did very well," the paper's then-publisher, Albert "Buck" Sherman, told Nieman Journalism Lab.[22] So the News took an unusual step: Print subscriptions were priced at $145 a year, print/online combos at $245 and online-only access would cost $345.

In other words, by forgoing the paper, a digital subscriber was on the hook for an additional $100. And Sherman wasn't coy about the rationale: "Our goal was to get people back into the printed product."

Some online-only content, such as videos and blogs, is outside the paywall; the same goes for columns like "Clergy Corner" and "Advice on Pets." But anyone who wants access to the electronic edition, which reproduces the day's paper, must pay. The company also operates a free site, newportri.com, designed to appeal to tourists and others looking for recreational or entertainment information.

In early 2011, the News dropped the price for print and online to $157, or a dollar a month above the print-only fee. But online-only access remains at $345—a price that current publisher William Lucey III says, in an interview, "is more of a deterrent." The amount was based on a scenario in which, "if everyone wanted only a digital product, this is what it would cost."

The paper's site, newportdailynews.com, gets around 80,000 visitors a month. Especially with online ad rates "dropping 20 percent a year," that's not enough to sustain the operation, which includes a newsroom of 22 people, Lucey says. Indeed, online ad revenue accounts for only 2 to 3 percent of total advertising for the paper.

After the change was put into effect, "our single-copy sales went up about 300 a day"—a bit less than 10 percent of overall single-copy sales. As the economy improves, "print is coming back. February [2011] was up 35 percent over last year" in ad sales.

And even with AOL's free Patch site moving into town, Lucey says there are no regrets. "We found our comfort zone, and we stopped agonizing about it." AOL, which launched the Patch site in Newport in July 2010, is sanguine: "The Newport Daily News does great work and has been a staple in Newport County for generations," says spokeswoman Janine Iamunno. "There is room for all of us."

*   *   *

So, which approach is best, free or paid?

Pay proponents often put it this way: High-quality journalism costs a great deal to produce, so users ought to pay to get it. Pay opponents have a counterargument: Paywalls cut sites off from "the conversation" online and will deprive them of the attention they need from blogs, aggregators and social media.

We prefer to frame it as a business issue—and in that respect, it's possible that neither side has it exactly right. In fact, pay plans may have little immediate impact on sites that are just getting into the business. The reason is that most companies are likely to have only small streams of online circulation revenue, which could roughly match advertising declines from lower traffic. Digital subscriptions may pay off in the years to come, but only if media companies can persuade consumers using new platforms—like smartphones and tablets—to adopt a pay plan.

Even before the Internet, subscription revenue didn't amount to much for most news organizations. Print publications often underpriced subscriptions because they believed they could lose money on circulation and make it up on advertising from larger audiences. Broadcast TV and radio were free, and fees for cable stations like CNN are buried in bills that make it impossible to discern the true costs of content. So in the old world, Americans weren't used to paying much for news; in the digital world, news organizations have spent 15 years training their consumers to be freeloaders.

As a result, most people are happy to pay nothing at all for news, even as they have come to accept paying for other forms of digital content. A 2010 study of 1,000 adults commissioned by AOL showed that about four in 10 people pay for "online content"—but that was a broad definition, including music and video.[23] Only 4 percent said they pay for online news. A Pew Project for Excellence in Journalism survey in January 2010 found little interest in paying: Among "loyal news consumers, only a minority (19 percent) said they would be willing to pay for news online, including those who already do so and those who would be willing to if asked."[24] Another Pew study in January 2011 showed 23 percent of respondents who say they would pay $5 a month to get full access to a local newspaper online; that dropped to 18 percent when asked if they would pay $10 per month.[25]

Some say such surveys miss the point. Porous pay systems like the New York Times' are being erected precisely so they will capture only the most devoted users. And a hypothetical question in a poll might not capture true sentiment. "Don't survey based on what people say they would pay," says Aaron Kushner, an investor who is mounting a bid to buy the Boston Globe from the New York Times Co. "No one expects to pay for news, so why would they answer differently?"

But even if pay schemes attract users, it's hard to charge enough to produce a great deal of revenue. Kushner argues that most publishers are making the same mistake now that they made years ago. "The problem is they're basing the price on cost or history rather than value. Forget pricing on cost," he says. If anything, he says, digital editions should be more valuable because of their archives and interactivity. "Figure out what is the value of the product and then price against it. Publishers have been undervaluing their product for too long."

There is, in some publishers' pay plans, an aura of frustration over the inability to convert large online audiences into advertising revenue. Moroney, of Dallas, is simply being more candid than most when he notes that much of the News' online ad space goes unsold, and so a cut in traffic to the site will have little financial impact. Others, such as Albert Sherman of the Newport Daily News, frame a paywall as a way to protect the print edition, but at most papers, some circulation has already been lost because of free alternatives.

The best chance to make headway with pay schemes is likely with a device that people can hold in their hands. For most mobile phones and tablets, a commerce system is already in place, and the transaction is straightforward. Moreover, consumers have shown a willingness to pay for content on mobile devices, whether that involves ringtones or sports videos. So, if publishers really hope to expunge the "original sin" of giving away content free online, they may be best positioned to do so not on the computers where they first gave away their wares, but on mobile devices that offer a more welcoming environment.

[1]   Stewart Brand, The Media Lab (Penguin, 1988), p. 202

[2]   John Lanchester, "Let Us Pay," London Review of Books, Dec. 16, 2010. http://bit.ly/h8gIt8

[3]   Bill Grueskin, "The Case for Charging to Read WSJ.com," guest post on Reflections of a Newsosaur blog, March 22, 2009. http://bit.ly/f2UB3x

[4]   Joel Meares, "Jim VandeHei talks Politico Pro," Columbia Journalism Review, Nov. 16, 2010, http://bit.ly/fSmKZb; see also Jeremy W. Peters, "Politico, Seeing a Market Need, Adds a Paid News Service," New York Times, Oct. 25, 2010. http://nyti.ms/hg1lPA

[5]   "Now Pay Up," The Economist, Aug. 27, 2009. http://econ.st/hJOUsM

[6]   David Smith, "Papers in U.S. losing readers; Democrat-Gazette gains subscribers," Arkansas Democrat-Gazette, April 27, 2010. http://bit.ly/fcoFs7

[7]   Information provided by Miami Herald circulation department.

[8]   "Old and New Media Go to Washington," from On the Media, NPR, May 8, 2009. http://bit.ly/hwsTyu

[9]   Transcript of remarks at Carnegie Corporation, provided by James Moroney.

[10] Justin Ellis, "Dallas Morning News publisher on paywall plans: 'This is a big risk,'" Nieman Journalism Lab, Jan. 6, 2011. http://bit.ly/eg0dSH

[11] "Annual Report and Accounts 2009," Pearson PLC. http://bit.ly/eO7Yfj

[12] FT's pricing plan details. http://on.ft.com/gY98fv. The FT's print circulation in 2011 was 381,658.

[13] "2010 Results Presentation," Pearson, Feb. 28, 2011. Slide 36, http://bit.ly/gXmf9p

[14] Bill Grueskin, "NYTimes.com Pay Scheme has a Great Big Hole," paidcontent.org, March 18, 2011. http://bit.ly/i5hyaZ

[15] The 85 percent figure comes from the Times' own story: Jeremy W. Peters, "The Times Announces Digital Subscription Plan," March 17, 2011. http://nyti.ms/hBJvt6

[16] One estimate says the Times was spending $40 million to $50 million: Brett Pulley, "New York Times Fixes Paywall Flaws to Balance Free Versus Paid on the Web" Bloomberg.com, Jan. 28, 2011, http://bloom.bg/fyCwLV. Publisher Arthur Sulzberger has said that's not accurate, and another journalist, Staci Kramer at paidcontent.org, put the price at $25 million: "New York Times Paywall Cost More Like $25 Million," http://bit.ly/fE71o2. Meanwhile, a former design director for the Times' site, Khoi Vinh, noted the opportunity cost for the Times in his post, "What the NYT Pay Wall Really Costs," subtraction.com, March 18, 2011, http://bit.ly/eHb6F9

[17] Staci D. Kramer, "The NYT Pay Plan's Most Dangerous Foe: Perception," paidcontent.org, March 27, 2011. http://bit.ly/dO7WdI

[18] Michael DeGusta, "Digital Subscription Prices Visualized (aka The New York Times is Delusional)," theunderstatement.com, March 21, 2011. http://bit.ly/hXON9f

[19] Lauren Kirchner, "Don't Call it a Paywall," CJR, April 6, 2011. http://bit.ly/f72MEa

[20] Tiernan Ray, "NY Times Sags; 100K Paid Digital Subs, and No Loss to 'Premium' Advertising," Barrons, April 21, 2011. http://bit.ly/fAHfjp

[21] Jonathan Landman, the Times' former deputy managing editor for digital journalism, quoted in Jeremy W. Peters, "The Times' Online Pay Model Was Years in the Making," New York Times, March 20, 2011. http://nyti.ms/ediOZO

[22] Edward J. Delaney, "Charging (a lot!) for news online: The Newport Daily News' new experiment with paid content," Nieman Journalism Lab, June 8, 2009. http://bit.ly/gtV5Hn

[23] "The Consumer and Content: Benchmark Study," AOL, September 2010. Slide 47 et al. http://bit.ly/fYAE1T

[24] "Economic Attitudes," State of the News Media 2010, Pew Research Center's Project for Excellence in Journalism. http://bit.ly/eA5DrX

[25] "Survey: Mobile News & Paying Online," State of the News Media 2011, Pew Research Center's Project for Excellence in Journalism. http://bit.ly/fsVAWf

Chapter 6

Aggregation: *'Shameless' – and Essential*

A group of middle school students at Brooklyn's Urban Assembly Academy of Arts and Letters got a special treat one March afternoon in 2011. Just five weeks after the announcement of the $315 million deal in which AOL acquired Huffington Post, AOL's chief executive, Tim Armstrong, and Arianna Huffington, HuffPost's co-founder, came to the school to teach a class in journalism.

The lesson—or what one could see of it in the short, treacly video account that ran on the Huffington Post—may have told more about the future of the news business than what either Huffington or Armstrong intended.[1] A few moments after the video begins, an official of the program that arranged the visit speaks to the camera: "We are delighted that Arianna Huffington and Tim Armstrong are going to be teaching a lesson on journalism." What the video showed, though, wasn't a lesson in how to cover a city council meeting, or how to write on deadline. Instead, the teacher in the classroom told her students, "We're going to give you headlines that we pulled from newspapers all over the place, and you guys are going to place them and decide what type of news they are."

This, then, was a lesson in aggregation—the technique that built Huffington's site up to the point that AOL wanted to buy it.

In just six years, Huffington has built her site from an idea into a real competitor—at least in the size of its audience—with the New York Times. The Huffington Post has mastered and fine-tuned not just aggregation, but also social media, comments from readers, and most of all, a sense of what its public wants. In the process, Huffington has helped media companies, new and old, understand the appeal of aggregation: its ability to give prominence to otherwise unheard voices and to bring together and serve intensely engaged audiences, as well its minimal costs compared to what's incurred in the traditionally laborious task of gathering original content.

HuffPost's model has provoked sharp criticism from, among others, Bill Keller, executive editor of the New York Times, who, like Captain Renault in "Casablanca," appears shocked that aggregation is going on.[2] "Too often it amounts to taking words written by other people, packaging them on your own website and harvesting revenue that might otherwise be directed to the originators of the material," Keller wrote. "In Somalia this would be called piracy. In the mediasphere, it is a respected business model." He wrote this even as the Times' own site has demonstrated the power of aggregation in many ways, notably in a blog called The Lede, which has deftly captured the tempo and texture of such ongoing stories as the protests in Iran and the upheaval in Egypt by blending Times reporting with wire reports and original material from outside sources.[3]

In fact, almost all online news sites practice some form of aggregation, by linking to material that appears elsewhere, or acknowledging stories that were first reported in other outlets. An analysis of 199 leading news sites by the Pew Project for Excellence in Journalism found that most of them published some combination of original reporting, aggregation and commentary and that the mix differed considerably depending on the management strategy, the site's history and—to be sure—its budget.

Pew categorized 47 of the sites it surveyed as aggregators/commentators and 152 as primarily producers of original content. In the aggregator/commentary group, fourth-fifths of the sites were online-only; of the original-content group, four-fifths were connected to traditional media.[4] Traffic is highly concentrated at the top of the list, with the top 10 sites accruing about 22 percent of total market share. Seven of the top 10 sites are "originators."[5]

What is surprising is that consumers use these different kinds of sites quite similarly. Original-content sites do marginally better at keeping visitors for longer stretches and leading them to more Web pages, but it is hard to imagine that this slightly higher engagement is enough to help cover the costs of original production and reporting.

Originators and aggregators

Primary content type	Number of top 199 news sites	Monthly visits per person	Web pages per person	Monthly time per person (min:sec)
Originator	152	3.93	16.00	12:36
Aggregator/ Commentary	47	4.23	15.86	12:06

SOURCE: Based on Nielsen NetView data of top sites, September to November 2009; discussed in "The State of the News Media 2010," Pew Project for Excellence in Journalism

Huffington often says that aggregation benefits original-content producers as much as it does the aggregators.[6] The story of a recent blog post on New York Magazine's site makes for a good illustration.

At about the time that Huffington and Armstrong were visiting the school in Brooklyn, Gabriel Sherman, a contributing editor to New York Magazine, was nailing down a scoop. Under the headline, "Going Rogue on Ailes Could Leave Palin on Thin Ice," Sherman reported that Roger Ailes, the head of Fox News, had warned his paid commentator, former Alaska Gov. Sarah Palin, not to go forward with her video accusing the media of "blood libel" in the way they portrayed conservatives after the shooting of Arizona Rep. Gabrielle Giffords.[7]

The story required at least three days of reporting and editing work. The facts had to be bulletproof. The post went live on nymag.com's Daily Intel column at 7:57 p.m. on March 13.

The next morning, an editor for the Huffington Post spotted the item and wrote a rendition of it for that site, publishing at 8:27 a.m.[8] Huffington Post played by the rules: It credited Sherman by name and gave nymag.com a link at both the beginning and the end of the item. What Huffington Post took from Sherman's post—237 words, or about half the original length—would be justifiable under almost any definition of copyright.

The power of aggregation soon became clear: The original Sherman post drew nearly 53,000 readers on nymag.com, and about 17,500 of them came directly from the links on Huffington Post. Smaller numbers of readers came from hotair.com, which is part of a network of conservative websites and publications; and from Andrew Sullivan's popular blog, The Daily Dish. All told, three-fourths of the traffic to Sherman's story came from other sites. The item also drew more than more than 130 reader comments on nymag.com, which is far higher than what the typical blog post gets.

The real winner, though, was Huffington Post. Its aggregated version of the item got more than 2,000 comments. Comments are not a perfect proxy for traffic, but it appears that the Huffington Post item got a much bigger audience for its post than the original New York Magazine item, for a fraction of the cost.

The power of aggregation

	Nymag.com Original reporting	Huffingtonpost.com Aggregated version
Date posted	March 13, 2011	March 14, 2011
Time posted	7:57 pm	8:27 am
Word count	463	237
Comments (as of April 21, 2011)	138	2,095

SOURCE: Nymag.com, Huffingtonpost.com

As this example shows, links from other sites or search engines are among the cheapest and most efficient ways to bring in new users. Even the largest news suppliers, such as Time.com or CNN.com, appreciate what top billing on You-Tube[9] or Google News can do to increase traffic and advertising revenue. "There are ways you can deliver better ad results, but you can't do it if you focus on your own content only and not others," Scout Analytics Vice President Matt Shanahan says. He adds that when sites promote each others' content, they create more engaged audiences through additional page views and commentary. "The advertiser wants the audience," he says. "And the audience wants the audience."

*   *   *

News organizations have always blended material from a variety of sources by combining editorial content from staff, news services, and freelancers; adding advertising; and then distributing the package to consumers. In the digital world, news aggregation is not so different. It involves taking information from multiple sources and displaying it in a readable format in a single place.[10] Digital aggregation businesses can be successful when they provide instant access to content from other sources, and they generate value by bringing content to consumers efficiently.

The cheapest way to aggregate news is through code and algorithms, with little or no human intervention. The way an individual story is displayed throughout the day is determined automatically, typically according to how recently the article was published and how popular it becomes. Aggregation is slower and more expensive when it becomes "curation," involving humans in the filtering and display processes.

Google News belongs to the most basic aggregation category, called "feed" aggregation, in which an algorithm sorts news by source, topic or story and displays the headline, a link and sometimes a few lines from the original story. The costs are low.

Yahoo News is an enhanced aggregation feed; it has always had some level of editorial management in the selection and placement of stories—though it posts up to 8,000 stories a day, so editorial involvement is fairly minimal. Like Google News, Yahoo News aggregates from across the Web, but it gives preference to the approximately 200 media companies from which it licenses content—such as the Associated Press, Reuters and ABC News. In return for the content, Yahoo News gives the partners a share of its ad revenue—in addition to sending them traffic.

Traffic to the news sections of Yahoo and Google is relatively small compared with the total traffic of these companies' sites. For example, in one week in April 2011, Yahoo News represented about 6.5 percent of the total traffic to all Yahoo sites as determined by the online audience measurement company Hitwise.[11] But Google News and Yahoo News are the first stop of the day for significant numbers of users, and that is considered a good predictor of multiple visits and customer loyalty. Yahoo and Google also let individual users customize their home pages by personal preferences—according to topic or news source. In the latest refinements, Yahoo has introduced a recommendation engine for stories called LiveStand, while Google introduced "News for You," which keeps track of what stories a user has clicked on and provides related content.[12] Large media companies such as the New York Times and Washington Post and independent companies like Flipboard are doing much the same thing—developing programs that can recommend stories and videos based on a user's previous choices. Because of the wide variety of topics and the enormous volume of stories posted, this is a far more difficult problem than creating the algorithms that Amazon or Netflix use for recommendations. Some companies are also working on adding friends' and networks' reading choices to the recommendation engine.[13]

On the other end of the spectrum, Huffington Post starts with algorithmic selections but puts them into the hands of human editors who set priorities for sections and then condense, rewrite or bring several organizations' versions of the same story together. HuffPost turbocharges the formula with a mix of social media, dynamic packaging, and photos and charts. These techniques lead to praise, criticism—and parody. Comedy Central's Stephen Colbert told viewers that, to retaliate for HuffPost's republishing without permission the entire contents of his show's website, he would create "The Colbuffington Repost," that is, the entire Huffington Post, just renamed. Its re-re-packaged content would make him the owner of the "Russian nesting dolls of intellectual theft."[14]

Newser.com, the aggregation site co-founded by Michael Wolff, represents much of what legacy media companies hate about the Web: It has little original reporting, and its stories are short rewrites of information from several other sites, with a design that emphasizes graphics. Wolff, a media critic who is now editor of Adweek, has spent much of his career playing provocateur—and driving people in the media business a little crazy. This effort is no different. Andrew Leonard, a writer for Salon, wrote a story called "If the Web doesn't kill journalism, Michael Wolff will." Leonard says that Newser displays a "truly precious degree of shamelessness. ... Even the slide shows are repackaged, rewritten and abbreviated versions of content originated by other publications."[15]

Newser says out loud in its slogan what many aggregation sites hope their users will infer: "Read Less, Know More." Its co-founder and executive chairman, Patrick Spain, says the site aims to limit its stories to 120 words. "The most time-consuming part of editorial is identifying which stories we are going to carry," he says. "And we have to identify the one, two, or three major sources to use to write the story." Wolff asks, "If you are a consumer, why would you go to a single source?" The New York Times, he says, "used to be seen as a broad view of the news" but is now regarded as "parochial and limited." Newser publishes about 60 stories, or digests of stories, per day, though it has at times published as many as 100. "Cost is less of a driver than the effect we are looking for," says Spain. "If you have hundreds of articles, it is not an editorial function; it is a fire hose function."

Newser has business offices in New York and Chicago, but its writers are free-lancers. They live in the U.S., Europe and Asia, and generally work from home. There are four full-time and about 15 part-time staff members who perform editorial duties, working at rates of $20 to $40 per hour. Spain says "this is a gigantic edit staff compared to Digg" (a site where story placement depends on readers' votes). "They have no editorial people. But this is tiny compared to the New York Times."

For its other functions, Newser has eight full-time employees who work on marketing, administration and management, and technology. Its total operating costs are about $1.5 million per year, for a site with 2.5 million unique visitors a month.[16] Spain and Wolff have both said that in 2011, they expect to break even—that is, to get to the point where advertising revenue is high enough to cover operating costs, though not to start paying back the initial investors.

Nymag.com does original reporting, as in the case of the Ailes/Palin story, but since 2007 it has also had a strategy of growing through four blogs that use third-party content combined with original reporting: Grub Street (on food), Daily Intel (political and media news), Vulture (culture) and The Cut (fashion). "These niches need editorial authority to be successful," said Michael Silberman, general manager of nymag.com. In a given week, the site publishes only about 35 articles from the print magazine but 450 to 500 blog posts and thousands of photos. As a result, only 14 percent of the site's page views are of content from the magazine. "Every time we increase the frequency of the blog posts, we can drive up the numbers of audience," Silberman says. And since 2007, nymag.com's audience has grown from 3 million unique users to 9 million.

The site has been particularly adept at going beyond its local roots. About 30 percent of the print magazine's audience comes from outside New York, but 70 percent of the website's readers live beyond the home market, which helps the site attract attracting national advertising. Its restaurant section, Grub Street, expanded in 2009 and is now in six cities.

The evolution of nymag.com's cultural news site, Vulture, from a small feature to a destination with 2.5 million unique users demonstrates how powerful aggregation strategies can be. When it started in February 2010, Vulture was getting 700 to 800 unique visitors daily. After its official launch in September 2010, Silberman found that it "filled an editorial hole in the marketplace." One of its most popular features is "clickables"—a stream of 20 short posts per day, featuring, among other things, viral videos and music albums leaked ahead of official release. Vulture now has 10 full-time editorial employees and get lots of support from New York Magazine back-office departments in finance, human resources and technology. The magazine has decided to spin off Vulture as its own site with a separate Web address sometime in 2011—a move that Silberman believes will help generate sales of entertainment and other national ads to companies that feel that a close tie to New York City can be an impediment.

*   *   *

There are few secrets on the Internet, and even fewer barriers to entry. Each innovation that works instantly attracts imitators and improvers. (LinkedIn, the professional networking site, launched LinkedIn Today in March 2011 to curate content not just by topic but also by what people in a user's network or industry are reading.[17]) Because aggregation is so much cheaper than original content, it has an automatic economic advantage, but the attractiveness of aggregation brings more and more competitors into the field. So merely being an aggregator is hardly a guarantee of economic security.

A few publishers have successfully sued sites that steal their content outright. That has led others to toy with the idea of getting news sites to unite and deny aggregators access to their content. Even if that kind of cooperation were legal— and it might not be—it would be impossible to sustain or enforce. There are just too many sites producing original content. The economic benefits of aggregation and being aggregated are significant, even if they differ widely from one site to the next.

---

[1]   Video, "Arianna and AOL CEO Tim Armstrong Teach Journalism Class At Brooklyn Middle School," Huffington Post, March 17, 2011. http://huff.to/i4ozzo

[2]   Bill Keller, "All the Aggregation That's Fit to Aggregate," New York Times, March 10, 2011. http://nyti.ms/htb7Xk

[3]   The Lede, New York Times. http://nyti.ms/hNf3xZ

[4]   The Project for Excellence in Journalism and the Pew Internet & American Life Project, "The State of the News Media: Nielsen Analysis." http://bit.ly/fflY0M "In making these categories PEJ looked at the front page of each site and counted the links on the site. If two-thirds of the links on the site were original content, the site was labeled an originator. If two-thirds of the links were to outside content, the site was categorized as an aggregator. Commentary sites are those that do not have original content in terms of original reporting, but have content that is mostly commenting or discussing reporting done by others."

[5]   Ibid.

[6]   One such example: Arianna Huffington, "Journalism 2009: Desperate Metaphors, Desperate Revenue Models, And The Desperate Need For Better Journalism," Dec. 1, 2009. http://huff.to/fEyZp1

[7]   Gabriel Sherman, "Going Rogue on Ailes Could Leave Palin on Thin Ice," nymag.com, March 13, 2011. http://bit.ly/hcqWRc

[8]   Jack Mirkinson, "Roger Ailes Told Palin Not To Make 'Blood Libel' Video: NY Mag," Huffington Post, March 14, 2011. http://huff.to/ieYDh9

[9]   "Tube Mogul Online Video Best Practices," December 2010. http://bit.ly/f426qV The average video featured on the YouTube home page gets 86,000 views per day.

[10] Kimberly Isbell, "What's the law around aggregating news online?" Nieman Journalism Lab, Sept. 8, 2010. http://bit.ly/hIXmUc The definition and distinctions among kinds of aggregation informed our discussion of these differences.

[11] "Top 20 Websites and Engines," Hitwise, April 16, 2011. http://bit.ly/frLcYt Hitwise is a company that measures online audiences using data aggregated from Internet service providers.

[12] "About the updates to Google News," Google News site. http://bit.ly/eh1tZI

[13] Erick Schonfeld, "Exclusive: An Early Look At News.me, The New York Times' Answer To The Daily," TechCrunch, Feb. 1, 2011, http://tcrn.ch/fb2KRw; Russell Adams, "Paper Starts New Website; Washington Post's Trove to Allow Readers to Build Custom Views of Online News," Wall Street Journal, Feb. 11, 2011. http://on.wsj.com/gbktyg

14 Video, "The Huffington Post Posts About the Colbuffington Re-Post," Colbertnation.com, Feb. 17, 2011. http://bit.ly/fyvimS

15 Andrew Leonard, "If the Web doesn't kill journalism, Michael Wolff will," Salon, April 5, 2010. http://bit.ly/gwfQXY The author also quotes other like-minded critics of Newser.

16 Traffic figures come from Omniture, which does census-based audience measurement for media companies

17 Press Release, "LinkedIn launches LinkedIn Today to deliver the news that matters most for professionals," LinkedIn.com, March 10, 2011. http://bit.ly/dHICXe

Chapter 7

Dollars and Dimes: *The New Cost of Doing Business*

Journalism is expensive and good journalism especially so, but the newsroom usually is not the costliest part of running a news organization. The Commerce Department has estimated that printing and delivery account for up to 40 percent of a newspaper's costs;[1] a 2007 study found that the newsroom accounts for only about 15 percent of a newspaper's expenses.[2] (One publisher reports that "infrastructure" costs—everything other than editorial and marketing—typically make up two-thirds of a newspaper's expenses.[3]) Still, editorial production has been a major expenditure, with newsroom costs running into the tens of millions of dollars even at mid-size news organizations, and far higher at major national news outlets. In 2008 the New York Times reported that its newsroom budget was more than $200 million per year.[4]

Such robust newsroom spending has been made possible, of course, by the information and advertising dominance that news media traditionally enjoyed. Outlets with 20 percent profit margins had the luxury of not having to think about the cost of each story produced. For decades, big-city newsrooms provided a wealth of resources to support top-tier reporting: newswires, clipping services, transcription services, research and library staff, and so on. A major investigative series might take months to prepare and cost tens of thousands of dollars, or even much more. (A New York Times editor estimated that the paper's collaboration with ProPublica on euthanasia in New Orleans hospitals after Hurricane Katrina cost $400,000; he later clarified that's what it would have cost if the Times had undertaken it alone.[5]) Even in a bare-bones newsroom, serious accountability journalism is not cheap, as the new generation of foundation-supported, online-only newsrooms can attest.

Consider CT Mirror, a nonprofit, online-only newsroom founded in 2010 to cover politics and government in Connecticut. It is hard to imagine a more sober outlet: CT Mirror focuses squarely on news about such topics as education, the economy, human services and the budget, with almost no human interest stories or even crime reporting. It is also hard to imagine a lower-cost outlet for serious reporting. CT Mirror is based in a modest Hartford office, and most of the seven-person editorial staff works from home or on the road. The site has no printing or delivery costs, and it has minimal sales or marketing expenses, and a simple, straightforward website; fully 75 percent of its foundation-provided budget goes to editorial salaries. "There's no room for fat," says founder and editor Jim Cutie.

Because CT Mirror is foundation-backed, it makes no secret of its budget. In its first 15 months of operation, the newsroom ran on $1.1 million in contributions and produced about 2,400 news stories, for an average cost per story of around $450. Similarly, the Gotham Gazette, a foundation-funded, nonprofit politics-and-policy news site based in New York City, has four employees and a $350,000 annual budget. It produces between four and eight original stories per week, for a per-story cost of more than $1,000.

Of course, not every item in a general-interest newspaper requires the same level of investment. One print daily, in a mid-size market with a relatively low cost of living, recently did an analysis to determine how much various articles cost. The newspaper, which shared its numbers on the condition it not be identified, found that the salary cost of reporting and writing stories ran from $190 to $430. The most expensive stories came from the opinion section, and the cheapest came from features. (The average cost per staff-written story was $227; articles by stringers cost $85.) Those figures don't include editing, production or distribution costs, which could easily triple the cost.

Meanwhile grass-roots local news sites such as Baristanet, in suburban New Jersey, and The Batavian, in upstate New York, operate on shoestring budgets. They keep costs at just thousands of dollars per month with tiny reporting staffs and almost no infrastructure. (See Chapter 3.) To replicate their cost structure would be difficult for a hard-news site like CT Mirror and all but inconceivable for a traditional, bricks-and-mortar newsroom working online as well as in broadcast or print.

This points to a central paradox of the online news economy: In an environment of sharply constrained ad revenue, the media's traditional economies of scale break down. What look like powerful editorial and business assets for online journalism—like established brands and well-staffed newsrooms—are turning out to be liabilities, because they are accompanied by a severe reduction in pricing power for circulation and advertising. The pressure on costs is intense.

One local TV station, interviewed for this report on the condition it not be identified, illustrates this paradox well. The station is a successful local broadcaster operating in one of the top four U.S. television markets. It has a 150-person news staff and is a leading source of local news in its market. For several years it has also operated a website, run by three dedicated producers who do original reporting as well as post stories and video drawn from newscasts.

On paper, the site has the assets to be a top online outlet for news about its city. It can draw on its sizable reporting resources and the promotional power of the station's broadcast operation. And it has free access to a large supply of valuable "rich media" assets in the video and audio segments produced by its parent.

The station has built a large online audience over the last several years, growing from a monthly average of 550,000 unique visitors in 2008 to about 2.5 million at the end of 2010. Still, the station's general manager has struggled to make the site break even. He shaved expenses substantially by outsourcing software and site maintenance and by cutting back on reporting from the field; not counting salaries, the site now costs roughly $500,000 per year to run. He has also tried a number of different sales strategies, including revenue-sharing partnerships and small, dedicated sites—"microsites"—custom-built for particular advertisers. Still, the site accounts for just 1 percent of the station's overall revenue. "Forget local being the holy grail," he says. "National sites are making money, but we don't have the scale locally to do so."

The cost pressure can be even more severe for local newspapers following their audiences to the Internet. A newspaper has enviable assets for putting news on the Internet—because it produces so much news text every day—and in theory it can also achieve enormous savings as it makes the switch to digital distribution, which does not require ink, paper and delivery trucks.

John Paton, chief executive officer of the Journal-Register Company, based in Yardley, Pa., has made reducing legacy costs the centerpiece of what he calls a "Digital First" strategy. The company, which came out of bankruptcy in 2009, owns 18 local dailies and scores of other "multi-platform products" across the Northeast and upper Midwest. Since becoming CEO in 2010, Paton has reduced expenses by consolidating printing facilities and outsourcing a wide range of noneditorial functions, from delivery to advertising design. He promises to have reduced infrastructure costs by 50 percent in three years.

Another prong of "Digital First" is to wean the publisher from its dependence on print advertising revenue, which Paton calls the "crack cocaine" of the business. He predicts that by the end of 2011, more than 15 percent of ad revenue will come from the digital side and that most of that will be purely online revenue—not ads sold in print-online package deals.

Paton has been a popular figure on the future-of-journalism circuit, appearing frequently at industry conferences to extol his company's digital gains. He frequently cites growth percentages for the Journal-Register site—for instance, he says the company's "digital audience" grew 75 percent in 2010, reaching 8.8 million unique visitors in March 2011. He also recently announced bonuses for employees and declared the company had made a $41 million annual profit.[6] It isn't clear, however, how that profit figure is calculated, because the company does not provide data on revenue, costs or other metrics as a publicly traded firm would. Paton says his investors don't want to disclose too much.

But Paton does acknowledge that moving revenue online amounts to "trading dollars for dimes"—or perhaps, if he's successful, quarters. The gamble is that the Journal-Register Co. will be able to cut costs and increase its online audience quickly enough to compensate for the lower revenue that online advertising brings.

The notion of "trading dollars for dimes" captures the impact of digital distribution on the economics of the business. Newspapers, magazines and broadcasting are all characterized by high fixed and low variable costs; it's quite expensive to produce the first copy of a newspaper, but it's far cheaper to produce the second copy—or the millionth. A local broadcaster faces much the same set of costs whether it reaches 100 viewers or 100,000. Hence the traditional media's profound economies of scale. News outlets that could not build a large enough base of readers or viewers to cover their steep fixed costs have tended to collapse in a few years, mired in debt. But those that surpassed that break-even point and went on to establish a mass audience could become immensely profitable—and those steep fixed costs created a natural barrier to competition.

Online, the equation changes dramatically. Observers sometimes underestimate the expense involved in running a high-quality, high-traffic online publication. But the barriers to entry are radically lower than in print or in broadcast. While a number of aspects of the online ad market have favored advertisers over publishers, simple audience fragmentation goes a long way toward explaining why news outlets have seen their revenue squeezed so tightly. Today, someone wanting political news or movie reviews has dozens of alternatives to choose from or stumble across.

A new curve for media costs online

On the Internet, the steep initial investment to launch a media business can be much smaller — but so are the profits (shaded areas) that come with increasing scale. An opportunity exists for small news sites with minimal costs; large newsrooms need to assemble far wider audiences than they did offline, or find ways to boost the revenue from each user.

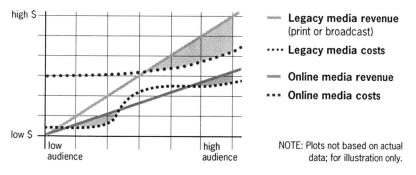

high $

low $

low audience

high audience

Legacy media revenue (print or broadcast)

Legacy media costs

Online media revenue

Online media costs

NOTE: Plots not based on actual data; for illustration only.

Thus both revenue and costs are lower online. To be more precise, the cost curve has been stretched out. The steep initial investment required to launch a media business is gone, and that has opened up opportunities for low-cost local or topical sites that aim to build an audience in the thousands or tens of thousands. This is the niche occupied by many moderately successful blogs as well as community sites like Baristanet, with modest ad income and even more modest expenses.

At the other extreme one finds large-scale media properties that have substantial technology or editorial costs but that amass enough sheer traffic to turn a profit. The dominant example here is Google, whose 175 million monthly users in the U.S.—generating billions of page views per month—allow it to capture more than 40 percent of the entire U.S. online advertising market.[7] Even considering only "display advertising" (that is, excluding search ads), Google accounts for 13 percent of ad spending. Yahoo and Facebook, the display ad leaders, each claim an additional fifth of the market.

However, most legacy news producers operate in the large and difficult middle of the cost curve, with traffic too low to compensate for the fixed expenses of news production, despite the savings that come from publishing online. In 2010, total operating expenses at the New York Times Co. ran to $2.1 billion, about two-thirds of the $2.9 billion total for Yahoo Inc.[8] Of course, somewhere between a third and a half of the newspaper's expenses would disappear if it no longer printed a paper edition. But Yahoo has many times more monthly visitors (roughly five times as many, if one counts traffic only to nytimes.com.). And while monthly visitors to all Times properties generate fewer than 2 billion page views, Yahoo serves out a staggering 100 billion pages each month.[9]

Justin Smith, president of Atlantic Media Co., argues that these dynamics explain both the opportunities the Internet affords and the stark challenge it has posed to established news providers. "There is a whole wave of new journalism models that have been developed at a fraction of the cost of traditional media," he says. "Traditional media players are way too set in their ways for reducing cost. They can't sustain the revenue to support their costs."

That is not to say, however, that any online venture that falls between a small community blog and Google is doomed to fail. In addition to running the Atlantic, Smith is a founder of Breaking Media, a collection of sites aimed at specific—and affluent—professional communities. Its properties cover law (Above the Law), Wall Street (Dealbreaker), fashion (Fashionista), green transportation (AltTransport) and accounting (Going Concern). Above the Law is the most successful of these sites, with a monthly audience of more than 700,000 unique visitors. Smith won't say when the company might turn a profit, but his formula depends on pulling together sizable audiences at minimal cost—each site has just two journalists, with ad sales and administration centralized.

Henry Blodget's Business Insider site is pursuing a similar strategy, on a much larger scale. Blodget has disclosed financial details about his media company, reproduced below, in what was an unusual move for a private firm.[10] "We're a private company, and we've never disclosed any of that stuff, either. But I'm honestly not sure why," he explained on March 7, 2011. "So we're going to try an experiment. We're going to disclose that stuff. Then we're going to see if something horrible happens to us."

Business Insider's intimate financials

	Feb 2011	Dec 2010	Dec 2009	Dec 2008
Site traffic (in 1000s)				
Estimated monthly uniques	7,800	6,000	2,600	2,000
Financials ($, 1000s)				
Gross revenue		4,800	2,000	700
Expenses		4,798	2,375	1,300
Operating income (loss)		2	(375)	(600)

SOURCE: Business Insider, March 7, 2011, and Henry Blodget

The statistics tell an interesting story. With 45 full-time employees, including 25 in the editorial department, Business Insider is hardly a grass-roots effort. In 2010 it cost almost $5 million to run. But unlike many sites of similar size, Business Insider managed to turn a tiny profit in 2010—about $2,127, or as Blodget put it, about enough to buy a MacBook Pro.

One factor accounting for Business Insider's survival is that the site targets investors and financial professionals rather than a general-interest audience. But that also means it must fight for readers and advertisers with the rest of the financial press, including giants like Bloomberg and Reuters and lower-cost sites like paidcontent.org and Breaking Media's.

The biggest difference between Business Insider and a similar site that doesn't break even is traffic: Blodget's venture managed to pull in 6 million unique visitors a month by the end of 2010, about double its audience of a year earlier. By March 2011, Business Insider had almost 8 million visitors, which represents a 30 percent jump in just three months. If the site becomes truly profitable, it will be by virtue of having continued that growth—getting to an audience of 15 million to 20 million visitors each month while keeping expenses flat.

The example of Business Insider suggests a provocative comparison with the old-media world. In the newspaper industry, a rule of thumb has been that every 1,000 additional readers justifies an additional newsroom employee. Going by Blodget's numbers, the comparable figure in online news media is closer to one person on the editorial staff per 150,000 readers.

As far as costs are concerned, then, the real advantage of digital-only operations, from The Batavian to Business Insider, is that they don't have to "trade dollars for dimes"—they are natives of the dime economy. By contrast, legacy news outlets must navigate a tricky cost transition when they go digital, cutting expenses and boosting online revenue while minimizing the damage to the traditional advertising that still sustains them.

This process begins by learning how to get the most out of their newsrooms in each medium. At the Atlantic, Justin Smith says, cost efficiencies depend on employees working across the digital/print divide. "There are very few employees who don't do both print and digital work," he says. "Maybe a couple of fact-checkers and one senior editor who concentrate on long pieces. We have about 60 people in editorial, and 99 percent of them are completely integrated." In advertising sales, all salespeople sell print and digital.

The Atlantic got a lot of attention in 2010 for having become profitable ("a tidy profit of $1.8 million"[11]) for the first time in decades. But the numbers disclosed were for the company as a whole, including print, digital and events. Still, Smith insists that the company's move to profitability depended on containing costs on the print side. "We were brutal about shifting resources away from print," he says. The company made layoffs in both the editorial and ad sales departments.

Does this mean the Atlantic makes money online? The company reported that digital advertising revenue rose 70 percent, and print advertising revenue 27 percent.[12] "The digital version of the Atlantic is definitely profitable," Smith says. "And it is a source of growing profit." Smith says this is the case even as the company continues to increase staff and resources on the digital side. The New York Times' report on the Atlantic had the magazine's overall revenue doubling, to $32.2 million in 2010, with advertising revenue accounting for about half of that. Digital ads supplied 40 percent of ad revenue.

For a large metro newspaper, the calculus of cost-cutting is tougher. Even in the face of declining readership and ad revenue, executives often fear that major cuts will only accelerate their slide in circulation.

Detroit is an exception. Newspaper executives there met early in 2008 to consider their options, none of which was very attractive. The Detroit area was on its way to a dead-last rating in a survey of 363 cities' job growth for the first decade of the 21st Century.[13] While most U.S. cities had one newspaper, Detroit had two—the Free Press and the News—bound in a joint operating agreement and dividing diminished circulation and ad revenue. (The agreement means that the two newsrooms compete, but their partnership handles both papers' ads, circulation and printing. The Free Press is owned by Gannett and the News by MediaNews Group; as part of a revised agreement, Gannett must pay MediaNews around $45 million over a 20-year period, according to Crain's.[14])

Then-publisher Dave Hunke assembled his team, and they kicked around ideas on how to cut costs. The ideas ranged from publishing a pocket-sized newspaper, to arming 200 citizen journalists with cameras, to a "dinner in a bag" promotion that would give special consideration to readers when they pick up meals at a local grocery store. The newspaper executives also considered deep reductions in staff or space devoted to news.

In the end, they came up with a radical idea: eliminating home delivery of both papers on Monday, Tuesday, Wednesday and Saturday. The reasoning was that those four days were responsible for only 23 percent of the papers' print ad revenue. The cutbacks went into effect in March 2009.

The four non-home-delivery days are now responsible for only 7 percent of the papers' print ad revenue. Those days' papers are smaller and are still sold as single copies in the city; several thousand are picked up by independent contractors who deliver them to houses, generally in Detroit's wealthier suburbs. The papers also have a same-day edition available by U.S. mail that reaches about 4,000 subscribers.

In October 2009, the dailies doubled their newsstand weekday price from 50 cents to $1. The cost of home delivery for Thursday, Friday and Sunday is now $13 a month, slightly less than what subscribers used to pay for seven days a week.

As part of the change, the companies launched an electronic edition for subscribers—basically a replica of that day's papers, available online. It loads slowly, though that has been improved since the early going. Access to the papers' websites remains free.

As a cost-cutting measure, executives say the move to three-days-a-week home delivery met their goals and helped stabilize their journalistic efforts. The company says the delivery change enabled it to trim its overall costs by 15 percent. "It ensured our survival," says Paul Anger, editor and publisher of the Free Press. Joyce Jenereaux, executive vice president of the Detroit Media Partnership, adds, "If we hadn't done it, we'd be putting out horrible products." But the bleeding hasn't entirely stopped. In November 2010, unions representing 900 employees got to look at internal financial data for the papers; after doing so, they agreed to pay cuts, a two-year wage freeze and increased health insurance payments.[15]

One thing that isn't clear is whether the Detroit strategy was successful in getting readers to move from print to digital platforms. As executives expected, circulation of the Detroit papers declined. In the months before the delivery change, the papers' combined weekday circulation was 436,238; in early 2011, that circulation was 230,876. Neither of those figures includes the e-edition, which has weekly traffic of more than 100,000. But the weekly e-edition number doesn't represent that many individual readers; someone who logs on five days in a row would be counted five times. Daily figures show that about 20,000 people visit the e-edition on each of the four days the paper isn't delivered, and that a third that many use it on days when the paper is delivered.[16] Engagement is substantial, as e-edition users spend about 18 minutes per visit. But the e-edition doesn't reach nearly as many people as used to get home delivery on the days that have been eliminated.

As for the papers' websites, they had significant growth in 2008—a year before the change in home delivery. That was a big news year which included the collapse of the auto industry, the historic Obama election and a scandal involving Mayor Kwame Kilpatrick's affair with his chief of staff. (The Free Press won a Pulitzer Prize for its coverage of the mayor's woes.) The papers grew 31 percent in unique users. After the cuts in home delivery, the number of users on the sites continued to grow, but more slowly: by 6 percent in 2009 and 10 percent in 2010.

Similarly, the year of big increases in time spent per visit on the Web was 2008, when it went from about 8 minutes to more than 13 minutes. Why? One reason, executives say, is that 2008 was the year that reader commenting was enabled on the site. "There was not a discernible bump when we made the model [delivery] change," says Patricia Kelly, senior vice president at Detroit Media Partnership. Kelly also notes that digital ad revenue is up 65 percent since 2005. Print advertising, meanwhile, is down 50 percent in the same period. As a result, digital is expected to represent an estimated 19 percent of total ad revenue in 2011.

The changes in the delivery model have affected the culture of the newsrooms to some extent. The papers' news staffs are designed to operate daily, just as before, without paying much attention to whether they are publishing in print or online on a particular day. Anger says, "It's everyone's responsibility to be invested in digital publication." But, says another editor, "There's still a feeling that, if you want people to see something, you're going to shoot for Thursday, Friday or Sunday. ... We haven't divorced ourselves from the idea that the big story should run on a day we publish a paper."

The deep cost-cutting measures by Detroit's dailies illustrate the challenge legacy news providers face as they adapt to the economics of online media. The strategy worked as a survival mechanism in a tough market; the damage from cutting home delivery was checked by the fact that print revenue is falling so quickly anyway. But it hasn't transformed a great number of print readers into new digital users. The sites' main growth occurred before the delivery change, and appears to have been fueled by big, well-covered stories, and improved functionality that got readers more involved.

---

[1] U.S. Department of Commerce, "The Emerging Digital Economy," April 1998. http://bit.ly/fLtcKX

[2] "Inland's 'Rules of Thumb' 2008," Inland Press, Sept. 8, 2008. http://bit.ly/eHlfkX

[3] John Paton, "Presentation at INMA Transformation of News Summit," Digital First, Dec. 2, 2010. http://bit.ly/dT0D3R

[4] Richard Pérez-Peña, "New York Times Plans to Cut 100 Newsroom Jobs," New York Times, Feb. 14, 2008. http://nyti.ms/ezJtN9

[5] Zachary M. Seward, "An extremely expensive cover story—with a new way of footing the bill," Nieman Journalism Lab, Aug. 28, 2009. http://bit.ly/fHZ8qU

[6] John Paton, "I Promised—You Delivered—The Checks Are Cut," Digital First, March 14, 2011. http://bit.ly/fFmdHp

[7] Heather Leonard, "Google's Share Of The Total Online Ad Market To Increase Even More," Business Insider, March 3, 2011. http://read.bi/hzajdl

[8] See The New York Times Company, "2010 Annual Report," Feb. 22, 2011. http://bit.ly/i4Zhxt and MarketWatch, "Yahoo! Reports Fourth Quarter 2010 Results," Jan. 25, 2011. http://bit.ly/hVBW1B

[9] Erik Schonfeld, "Facebook Now Has Yahoo In Its Sites, Already Bigger In Pageviews," TechCrunch, Feb. 1, 2010. http://tcrn.ch/gKquzo

[10] Henry Blodget, "BUSINESS INSIDER SECRETS REVEALED: An Inside Look At Our Readership And Financial Performance," Business Insider, March 7, 2011. http://read.bi/gDGml9

[11] Jeremy W. Peters, "Web Focus Helps Revitalize The Atlantic," New York Times, Dec. 12, 2010. http://nyti.ms/fSxPEJ and Matt Kinsman, "The Atlantic Posts Profit for First Time In Years," Folio, Jan. 6, 2011. http://bit.ly/eCrPt2

[12] Jeremy W. Peters, op.cit.

[13] United States Conference of Mayors, "U.S. Metro Economies: GMP—The Engines of America's Growth," June 2008. http://bit.ly/gzYWRy

[14] Bill Shea, "Free Press, News struggle after revising their JOA," Crain's Detroit Business, Aug. 1, 2010. http://bit.ly/i2v8GX

[15] Bill Shea, "Newspaper unions at Detroit dailies ratify two-year contract," Crain's Detroit Business, Nov. 15, 2010. http://bit.ly/hBW9Yo

[16] Figures provided to the authors by Detroit Media Partnership.

Chapter 8

New Users, New Revenue: Alternative Ways to Make Money

"The basic point about the Web is that it is not an advertising medium, the Web is not a selling medium, it is a buying medium. It is user-controlled."
—Jakob Nielsen, Web usability expert, 1998[1]

The journalism business these days often seems like a strange new world. As Jack Sweeney, who has been the publisher of the Houston Chronicle since 2000, puts it, "I thought I knew this business, and I did. But this business-model blowup is totally different." Sweeney has had a long career with newspaper advertising departments in Washington, D.C., Trenton, N.J., and Boston,[2] and he could have been talking about a number of the efforts news organizations are making to grow—like a Utah TV station's classified-ad service that has turned into a community resource, or a national media company selling ads that never appear on its own sites, or his own initiative as a service provider to small businesses. The tactics differ, but they share a common strategy: News companies are developing new businesses, not just propping up the old ones. And in doing so, they are challenging some of the orthodoxies that had slowed their transition to the digital world.

For most of these companies, the revenue from such new initiatives is modest; it doesn't begin to replace the dollars lost in the traditional business. But there are encouraging signs. The process of finding new readers and dollars is forcing media companies to redefine who they are and what business they are really in.

*   *   *

Sweeney makes his point with a spreadsheet that shows how much some of Houston's biggest retailers spent in 2010 on ads in the Chronicle. The numbers aren't what they used to be, and he knows they're not coming back. Even though the Chronicle remains the country's 10th-largest newspaper, its circulation dropped by more than 10 percent in 2010 over the year before, to 343,952. A decade ago, it was nearly 550,000.[3] Moreover, online display advertising, which was just under $28 million in 2010, won't make up the difference on its own, as it represents 12 percent of total ad revenue.

So the Chronicle, with guidance from its owner, Hearst Corporation, is looking to a sector often ignored by big media—the small fry. "We didn't used to go after mom-and-pop businesses," Sweeney says. "Houston has 310,000 businesses with 10 employees or less. The potential is huge. As department stores have consolidated, we needed something new."

What makes the Chronicle's approach interesting is that it isn't based on selling ads that appear on the pages of the site or in the newspaper. Instead, the Chronicle is launching a consulting business—selling a host of Internet services, from website design to improving businesses' rankings on search engines. And when the Chronicle does sell ads as part of this outreach, those are just as likely to appear on Yahoo or Facebook as on chron.com.

To get started, Sweeney hired about 30 employees, some of whom who knew the world of small businesses from having worked at Yellow Pages. The Chronicle also retrained some of its own staff. The sales pitch it makes to businesses is this: The Chronicle evaluates their websites, improves their rankings on search-results pages and helps them write press releases that are posted on the chron.com site to give traffic a boost.

The Chronicle charges $500 and up a month for the service, asking its clients to sign one-year contracts. As of April 2011, the fourth month of the program, it had enrolled nearly 500 businesses and booked more than $2.5 million in contracts. Sweeney's goal is to reach around $7 million in annual revenue.

Others are also in this business. One firm, ReachLocal Inc., signed up nearly 17,000 advertisers, booking nearly $300 million in revenue in 2010.[4] McClatchy has partnered with Webvisible, a California-based Web services firm that says it has more than 10,000 clients.

But even if the effort is as successful as the Chronicle hopes, Sweeney figures it would do no more than match the current revenue from one of the paper's biggest advertisers. In other words, it will be a big help but is not, in itself, a replacement for the old business model. "This has become a nickel-and-dime business," he says. "And you need a lot of nickels and dimes."

*   *   *

A decade ago, KSL, a local TV station in Salt Lake City, came up with what was then a novel idea: It would start its own classified-ads section on KSL.com and end its relationship with a company that was already providing that service for the site.

"We were making like $300,000 a year [in revenue] on the partnership, which back then was a lot of money online," says Clark Gilbert, president and chief executive officer of Deseret Digital Media. But the station, an NBC affiliate, saw the change as a way to build traffic to the site. Its classifieds service would also be a way to showcase the moral standards of its owner, the Church of Jesus Christ of Latter-day Saints. Deseret Digital Media runs the online properties for the church's TV station and its newspaper, the Deseret News, along with sites more obviously of the church, MormonTimes.com and DeseretBook.com.

Today, KSL.com is a powerhouse on the Web. The site has more than 4 million unique users and generates an astounding 250 million page views a month, says Gilbert. (KSL's sister property, the Deseret News, has a more typical audience of about 2.5 million unique users and 30 million page views; the website of a competing newspaper, the Salt Lake Tribune, has roughly the same size audience.) In a recent study of Web traffic data in major markets, a company called Internet Broadcasting found that KSL.com reaches 48.8 percent of its local market. That is more than any local media outlet in the survey but one, the Minneapolis Star Tribune's site. And it is far beyond the Web footprint of the top local TV stations, which average under 20 percent market share.[5]

Still, all that traffic didn't keep Deseret Digital Media from announcing lay-offs last year at the Deseret News[6] that, despite the sunny headline that announced the news ("Deseret News set to lead, innovate"), resulted in a cutback of 43 percent of the newspaper's workforce and consolidation of some news-gathering operations with KSL-TV.[7] (The Salt Lake Tribune announced the layoffs with some competitive schadenfreude: "Tribune to press ahead in face of News changes."[8])

KSL.com's strategy relies partly on its worldwide audience of church members, but it also offers useful lessons for news organizations seeking untraditional ways to build a digital audience.

The classifieds themselves are mostly free, though advertisers can pay up to $10 a day to get prominent placement. The classifieds pages also host other ads, and more importantly, they are responsible for about 70 percent of KSL.com's total traffic, so they provide tremendous benefits to the rest of the site. The pages carry prominent links to news stories and videos on KSL.com, which helps to generate 70 million to 80 million page views a month for content that isn't classified ads. "The main route to the site is still the news page," Gilbert said. "We haven't tried to make 'KSL.com/classifieds' our bookmark. That made the [KSL] news site bigger than any other news site in the market."

Gilbert adds that there is another benefit: "Here's something hard for old-media people to accept. ... Our news content gave a level of trust to the classifieds, and classifieds drove relevance back to the news." Or, put another way, the fact that readers have come to rely on the classifieds under the KSL brand helped to build relevance and credibility in the news as well.

KSL.com had some important advantages. First, it started early, shortly before Craigslist came to Salt Lake City. And because it was a TV station's website, it wasn't perceived as competitive by its existing staff; there was no classified-ads manager to complain about giving away a lucrative revenue stream. "KSL didn't have legacy products that were competing with this service," says Chris Lee, general manager of DeseretNews.com. "If they wanted to do cars, there wasn't someone saying, 'But we're already doing cars!'"

The site also demonstrated a keen sense of its audience—which shouldn't be a surprise, given the church ownership. Managers tried to be especially vigilant about keeping the site clean ("no way were we going to allow prostitute or massage ads," Gilbert says) and detecting fraud.

KSL.com also committed to "letting our users develop the product with us," Gilbert said. For instance, in the spring of 2011, KSL.com asked its readers what kinds of firearms they thought the site should allow to be sold. It also asked them, "How often do you believe people are using the KSL Classifieds Firearms and Hunting section to circumvent firearm laws?"[9] Users help police the site for bad actors. Anonymity isn't allowed: "Sellers had to have an identity," Gilbert said.

The classifieds give KSL.com an unusually high level of engagement. According to Mike Petroff, vice president of new media sales, the site gets around 10 million page views from 250,000 users on an average weekday, for a stunning daily rate of 40 page views per visitor. (The ads don't appear on the newspaper's site; the Deseret News shares business, but not newsgathering, operations with the Salt Lake Tribune, owned by MediaNews Group.)

Most ads expire after 30 days. Even with such a short lifespan, there were more than 206,000 listings on a typical day in March 2011, in categories ranging from goats to muzzleloaders, from paintball equipment to bands seeking members.

Gilbert came to Salt Lake City in late 2009 after a career that included a professorship at Harvard Business School, where he worked closely with Clayton Christensen, author of "The Innovator's Dilemma," a well-known book about disruptive change.[10] The two of them collaborated on the "Newspaper Next" project, a 2006 study sponsored by the American Press Institute to encourage innovation.[11] Gilbert was hired by Deseret Management Corp.'s president and chief executive officer, Mark Willes, who had a troubled reign as CEO of Times Mirror (1995-2000) and publisher of the Los Angeles Times (1997-1999).[12]

One of Gilbert's main goals was reflective of a tenet of Christensen's philosophy: "Business units don't evolve; corporations do."[13] So Gilbert separated the digital sales force to enable it to take more risks. He said that KSL.com had been "run through the mainline channel—the TV. The [ad] sellers would have an afterthought to also sell Web. They'd throw it in if you also bought TV." The new company "created a profit-sharing relationship with the legacy organization. They'd benefit from our growth—but they didn't control it."

KSL.com's revenue grew 75 percent from 2009 to 2010, executives say, though they don't spell out numbers.[14] Gilbert says his company will continue to push on both the cost and the revenue sides of the equation: "News is expensive," he says, and audience loyalty is key. "You can't get two clicks and expect to pay off on that investment."

*   *   *

For decades, there has been a connection between the journalism that news organizations provide and the advertisements that generate most of their revenue. Whether it's a glossy spread that runs before the table of contents in a fashion magazine, or the anchorman's "more after this message" assurance on the local Eyewitness News, ads and content have always been closely linked in the stream that appears before the consumer.

That linkage is breaking down, and news organizations are scrambling to replace it with something else. That may mean selling ads on sites they don't own or control. "Creating content doesn't ensure a well-sized audience," says Chris Hendricks, vice president of interactive media at newspaper chain McClatchy Co. "We're accepting of the fact that the two may be disengaged." He then adds something one wouldn't have heard a few years ago from a media executive: "The longstanding premise of content and advertising being inextricably linked has clearly fallen apart."

McClatchy and other companies are turning toward selling advertising space on other sites, including Facebook and Yahoo. "It's almost like we are a sales and distribution company that decided we're going to fund journalism," says Hendricks.

Salespeople at McClatchy's 30 daily newspapers, as well as those at many other news organizations, sell ads on Yahoo as part of their pitch to local advertisers. For a worldwide company like Yahoo, "it's very difficult and expensive to set up a local sales force of size," Hendricks says. In the 1990s, Microsoft tried and failed to crack the market with a venture called Sidewalk, which was designed to produce city guides and sell local ads. Hendricks notes that Yahoo's rates for local ads tend to be higher than for national ads—but Yahoo needed people who knew the communities and businesses. "So we became their local sales force selling their inventory."

Because Yahoo has such broad reach, the relationship opens a big market for local news organizations. "The typical paper has 15 percent penetration in the local market," Hendricks says, speaking of online operations. "When we partner with Yahoo, it takes us up to 80 percent." And because many Yahoo ads are "behaviorally targeted"—meaning they are more closely geared to readers' interests, based on Web usage habits, geography or demographics—the rates are much higher. But those ads need a lot of viewers to ensure that the subsections of the audience are big enough to interest advertisers. "It's almost impossible to sell behaviorally targeted ads with 15 percent penetration," Hendricks says. "With Yahoo's scale you can." McClatchy averages an $18 cost per thousand views for targeted ads, Hendricks says. That's about twice the average for its usual display ads, though it has to share the proceeds with Yahoo.

There are longstanding examples of moves to sell inventory beyond a company's sites, including careerbuilder.com, an employment-classified site that McClatchy jointly operates with Gannett and Tribune companies.[15] But there can be difficulties. It isn't easy to persuade traditional ad departments to sell inventory that is not their own. "The gravitational pull of print is very strong. As soon as you get away from distribution and content adjacency, the harder it gets," Hendricks says. And ad sales on other sites represent only a small revenue stream so far. Hendricks says McClatchy sold about $15 million of Yahoo ads in 2010 and expects to increase that to as much as $19 million in 2011. To put that into perspective, as dismal as 2010 was for McClatchy, the company still sold a billion dollars of advertising that year.[16]

*   *   *

One of the issues in selling others' ad space is that a publisher must adjust to a variety of pricing schemes. For example, the Houston Chronicle tells advertisers that it can help them reach, say, local men between the ages of 25 to 64 on Facebook. But Facebook users would need to see an ad 2,500 times before the advertiser could be assured it would generate a single click, according to the Chronicle. That's a key reason that the price of ads on Facebook is low: $1,500 for 1.875 million impressions on Houston's rate card, or a CPM of just 80 cents, less than a tenth of what most news sites get. Others have calculated Facebook's effective CPMs as even lower, below 20 cents.[17] By comparison, for targeted ads on Yahoo Sports or Finance, the Chronicle expects to charge up to $4,400 per 200,000 impressions, for a CPM of $22.

Actual ad costs often vary from what appears on a rate card as a result of bargaining between buyer and seller. Nevertheless, it's noteworthy that the Chronicle charges nearly 28 times as much for ads on Yahoo as on Facebook. The price difference is a result of several factors, including the more prominent display space on Yahoo and the problems that social-media sites like Facebook have getting users to see or click on ads. In November 2010, the Wall Street Journal reported that 24 percent of all online display ads in the U.S. now appear on Facebook, but that they are responsible for less than 10 percent of total display-ad revenue.[18]

Why do Facebook ads get such low rates? And what does that mean for the rest of the market? It could be that the standard ways of valuing advertising—that is, by whether it will impel a consumer to buy a product, visit a store or feel better about a brand—simply don't work very well in a world where people using social media aren't looking to be sold something.

In a prescient 2008 AdAge column, Matthew Creamer summed up an issue that runs throughout this discussion: "The Internet is too often viewed as inventory, as a place where brands pay for the privilege of being adjacent to content. …The presumed power of that adjacency has provided the groundwork for the media industry for decades."[19] Companies today have faster and cheaper access to consumers. "The marketer, once at the mercy of a locked-up media landscape, can now be a player in it," he adds.

Inevitably, as Creamer notes, the discussion becomes one of how marketing is shifting to "earned" media rather than paid. One analyst defines the distinction this way: "'Earned media' is an old PR term that essentially meant getting your brand into free media rather than having to pay for it through advertising," writes Sean Corcoran of Forrester Research. "The term has evolved into the ... word-of-mouth that is being created through social media."[20]

If marketers believe they can reduce their advertising costs by engaging consumers directly, that almost certainly cuts revenue for news organizations. Although some firms are trying to capitalize on the trend by assisting advertisers with their social-media strategies, that is a labor-intensive business that is outside the expertise of many media companies.

And there are journalistic problems that go beyond the economic loss represented by the decline of old-fashioned advertising relationships. A Florida company, Izea, explicitly sets up arrangements so people who blog or tweet favorably about a company can get compensated in cash, travel or in other ways. The company insists that its writers adhere to Federal Trade Commission guidelines, enacted in 2009, requiring disclosure of "'material connections' (sometimes payments or free products) between advertisers and endorsers."[21]

But a 2010 study by Izea found that many people engaged in this "social media sponsorship" weren't aware of the FTC guidelines or had been offered compensation without a requirement to disclose it. The survey respondents also priced a "sponsored tweet" from a personal Twitter account at an average of $124 and a "sponsored blog post" at $179—around the same amount a small news organization will pay for a story and far more than an average blog post would ever get from display ads.[22]

* * *

None of these ventures comes close in potential payoff to the online coupon craze, pioneered most successfully by Groupon. The company was launched in Chicago in November 2008, offering its customers daily discount deals on services ranging from nail salons to restaurant meals. For the deals to kick in, a minimum number of users must sign up; the system encourages users to spread the word and to take advantage of social media.

In a little over two years, the company expanded to more than 500 markets in 44 countries and turned down a $6 billion takeover offer from Google. Forbes called it "the fastest-growing company in Web history."[23]

The company's model is a repudiation of much of what has driven online revenue for media companies. "Banner ads seem such a relic of the 19th century," Groupon founder Andrew Mason told Wired.com. "If God created man and the Internet on the same day, we would see more stuff like Groupon."[24]

The company has drawn complaints, particularly from retailers like some Chicago restaurant owners who said many Groupon customers either came only for the discount and didn't return, or gamed the system by copying coupons and using them repeatedly.[25] Groupon has also spawned a host of competitors.[26] And media companies have wavered between joining with Groupon or competing with it.

The Minneapolis Star Tribune launched a coupon service, called STeals. Cox Media has started DealSwarm. McClatchy is trying to have it both ways: It announced a deal with Groupon in July 2010.[27] Less than a year later, McClatchy said it would launch its own deal service, while continuing to work with Groupon. As AdAge noted, "McClatchy gets 15% of revenue from Groupon deals … on its own, McClatchy could collect as much as 50% from deals it sells and distributes."[28]

But it may be too late for news organizations to get substantial revenue from this business. Groupon is reported to be considering an initial public offering that could raise as much as $15 billion.[29] With so much capital, Groupon could compete on price and breadth in ways that would overwhelm ordinary competitors. And Groupon has its own challenges. It is possible that so many competitors' coupons will flood the market that consumers and businesses will begin to tune them out, which would diminish the value of the idea.

*   *   *

Many media companies are trying to raise revenue through more untraditional means. Wired Magazine opened a physical "Wired Pop Up Store" in New York City during the winter holidays, where it holds events like a "Geek Dad Family Party."[30] The store sells gadgets and paraphernalia. New York Magazine sponsors a wedding showcase event every year, selling tickets to the public, and sponsorships to national fashion brands; it also caters to local disc jockeys, dress stores, bakeries and other enterprises in the wedding business.

Such events may be good for branding, but tend not to bring in a great deal of new revenue. The Atlantic is different. It is involved in running about 75 events a year, the most ambitious of which is the Aspen Ideas Festival. "Most magazines do events for advertisers," says Justin Smith, president of the Atlantic Media Group. "We use the Atlantic brand and editorial prowess for attracting people." The business, called Atlantic LIVE, also runs events with such names as the Green Intelligence Forum and the Food Summit. They usually include partnerships with organizations tied to the topic. Coverage of the event may appear on the Atlantic's site or in the pages of the magazine.

Atlantic LIVE is run separately from the magazine and website and has its own sales group and editors who run the events. It has become a significant source of income for the company. Of the $32 million reported as revenue by the company in recent publicity, as much as $6 million comes from these events.

*   *   *

If the old formula of "adjacency"—selling ads and commercials alongside content—is fading, what will replace it? There are many possibilities, but few are likely, on their own, to provide the stream of dollars that advertising and circulation once did.

It may be most useful to resist the temptation to think about digital journalism economics in terms of moving an old business model to a new realm. The common thread in the strategies described in this chapter is that they demonstrate an embrace of the Internet, rather than an attempt to subjugate it to legacy business models.

When viewed that way, the Internet isn't a friend or an enemy. It's reality.

---

[1]   "The Web Is Not a Selling Medium," Art Bin, August 1998. http://bit.ly/eQcBwa

[2]   Sweeney's bio is at http://bit.ly/i06QiK

[3]   Jeremy Peters, "Newspaper Circulation Falls Broadly but at a Slower Pace," New York Times, Oct. 25, 2010, http://nyti.ms/ey8hHC and AdAge circulation data, http://bit.ly/fwgh8k

[4]   "ReachLocal Reports 44% Annual Revenue Growth for 2010," ReachLocal website, Feb. 15, 2011. http://bit.ly/fdkpSK

[5]   "Local Media Reach: 2010," Internet Broadcasting, Jan. 26, 2011. http://bit.ly/eWo2SF

[6]   Sarah Jane Weaver, "Deseret News set to lead, innovate," Deseret News, Sept. 1, 2010. http://bit.ly/ewGLJy

[7]   Ibid.

[8]   Tom Harvey, "Tribune to press ahead in face of News changes," Salt Lake Tribune, Aug. 31, 2010. http://bit.ly/es3QnY

[9]   KSL.com firearm survey was active in March and April 2011 at http://bit.ly/hO809N

[10] "DMC unveils new digital media and broadcast operating divisions," KSL.com, Sept. 10, 2009. http://bit.ly/fQkmjg

[11] "Newspaper Next: Blueprint for Transformation," American Press Institute, 2006. http://bit.ly/iewNO8

[12] Felicity Barringer, "A General Whose Time Ran Out," New York Times, March 15, 2000. http://nyti.ms/hRArcp

[13] "Disrupting Class: How Disruptive Innovation Will Change the Way the World Learns," Dec. 3, 2009. http://bit.ly/hPlWln

[14] "Clark Gilbert's Session at Borrell Associates' Local Mobile Advertising Conference 2010—Dallas, TX," Borrellassociates.com, http://bit.ly/fBlSFD; Gilbert speaks about KSL.com's revenue around 14:30 into the video. The figure has since been updated by the company.

[15] CareerBuilder: Profile—History. http://cb.com/fhfMTe

[16] Press Release, "McClatchy Reports Fourth Quarter 2010 Earnings," Feb. 8, 2011. http://bit.ly/hsfERQ

[17] "Facebook advertising metrics and benchmarks," go-Digital Blog. http://bit.ly/gMwxsw

[18] Geoffrey A. Fowler and Emily Steel, "Valuing Facebook's Ads," WSJ.com, Nov. 11, 2010, http://on.wsj.com/faZueN Advertisers have posted click-through stats on a Facebook chat page. The comments from 2010 and 2011 show varied results: One user said his ad drew 674 clicks out of 320,000 impressions, for a rate of about one click per 475 impressions. Another got one click in 2,480 impressions. Another was one per 1,818. See "Share your experience with Facebook ads (CTR, CPM, etc)," Facebook chatboard. http://on.fb.me/gfd0wI

[19] Matthew Creamer, "Think Different: Maybe the Web's Not a Place to Stick Your Ads," Advertising Age, March 17, 2008. http://bit.ly/fQrJwV

[20] Sean Corcoran, "Defining Earned, Owned And Paid Media," Forrester Blogs, Dec. 16, 2009. http://bit.ly/dMR8sE

[21] "FTC Publishes Final Guides Governing Endorsements, Testimonials," Federal Trade Commission website, Oct. 5, 2009. http://1.usa.gov/hh1meg

[22] "Twitter Users and Bloggers Open to More Than Earned Media," eMarketer, Sept. 22, 2010. http://bit.ly/feLdMh. Original study was sent to authors by Izea.

[23] Christopher Steiner, "Meet The Fastest Growing Company Ever," Forbes, Aug. 30, 2010. http://bit.ly/h0qQwf

[24] Ryan Singel, "Startup Hits Sweet Spot for Selling Local Services," Wired.com, Nov. 4, 2009. http://bit.ly/egnGnt

[25] "Groupon Faces More Criticism After Flower Deal, Unhappy Restaurants," MyFoxChicago.com, Feb. 15, 2011. http://bit.ly/e62Kg7

[26] Sarah Hartenbaum, "Deals Galore, Competitors Abound: A Primer On Groupon-Like Startups," TechCrunch.com, July 11, 2010. http://tcrn.ch/hfAC5V

[27] David Kaplan, "McClatchy Makes A Deal With Social Shopper Groupon," paidcontent.org, July 1, 2010. http://bit.ly/fXe9Q2.

[28] Kunur Patel, "McClatchy, a Groupon Partner, Starts Selling Its Own Daily Deals, Too," AdAge, March 23, 2011. http://bit.ly/fs4tgt

[29] Evelyn M. Rusli and Andrew Ross Sorkin, "Groupon Advances on I.P.O. That Could Value It at $15 Billion," NYTimes.com, Jan. 13, 2011. http://nyti.ms/gBo4xL

[30] Photo gallery of 2010 Wired store: http://bit.ly/gshwh6

Chapter 9

Managing Digital: *Audience, Data and Dollars*

Although all digital news organizations live in a brutally competitive environment, some companies do much better than others because their managers respond more deftly to opportunities.

Arianna Huffington is in that category, and the Huffington Post's growth in audience[1] and influence[2] is an example of a sustained idea and management attention. The venture capitalist Eric Hippeau was an early investor and was CEO of the site for several years, until its sale to AOL in February 2011. He was struck by the conviction of the founders—Huffington and Ken Lerer, a corporate communications executive turned venture capitalist—that much of U.S. society had lost trust in authority and in journalism. When Huffington Post launched in 2005, blogs were resonating with consumers. "They didn't have to go through gatekeepers—journalists," Hippeau said. "Blogs could democratize news." Logically flowing from this idea was a focus on encouraging reader commentary, and HuffPost hired people to help ensure that the conversation would be democratic and open.[3] "It is expensive to moderate," Hippeau said. "We have 25 full-time in-house moderators."

What HuffPost's founders didn't know at the beginning was how rapidly social media were going to grow. After all, in 2005, YouTube was just getting started and Facebook was still confined to colleges and universities. But HuffPost's management quickly realized that the social media trend fit with their original convictions. "As the audience embraced social media, we followed, " said Hippeau. And that attention to engaging readers—who now contribute 4 million comments a month on the site—led them to spend more on technology and less on content.

Huffington Post also developed an ability to respond quickly to the data that it was getting on traffic and usage—something that is a crucial component of success in digital journalism. Indeed, data analysis has moved from being a required skill in media companies' finance departments to being an essential part of the résumé for editors, writers and designers.

At CNNMoney.com, "Everyone on the staff has access to page-view and traffic data," says Executive Editor Christopher Peacock. The staff gets daily emails listing the top 50 stories by section as well as by the entire site. And, he says, "We have real-time metrics. We have a proprietary system to tell us how engaging our headlines and home page are."

LIN Media, with its 32 local TV broadcast stations, has an integrated content-management system that distributes content (and allocates costs) across all its markets and platforms. Its daily report on the previous day's metrics is sent around to business and editorial departments each morning. "Sometimes this report affects broadcast TV decisions as well," says Robb Richter, senior vice president for new media. "It's like having a great focus group all day long."

Forbes Chief Product Officer Lewis DVorkin writes a blog about the company's evolving business practices, often noting the integration of previously independent departments, functions and platforms at the company. DVorkin sees this integration as essential to Forbes' digital growth. "The Web and social media turned everything upside down. Knowledgeable content creators, audience members and marketers, too, now possess tools to independently produce and distribute text."[4] Expanding readership, once the job of circulation experts, is now done by business and editorial employees who develop "audience growth strategies," which shape coverage. When they decide which topics (say, college tuition) are likely to attract more readers, or different readers, that affects the recruitment of bloggers, and the efforts of staff and contributors to find followers and fans.

Forbes also encourages its largest advertisers to contribute content directly to the magazine and the site as part of their advertising buy. The companies are given tools to publish content—text, video and photos—on their own page on the site. This might startle journalists who expect strict separation between the editorial and business sides, but DVorkin sees this effort as a logical way to bring in advertisers who know they can create digital content elsewhere, through websites and email. Labeling the material as coming from advertisers helps inoculate the company from violating the church-state divide, DVorkin says, adding that Forbes' approach allows marketers not to be confined in the "ghetto" of freelance-written advertorial. The advertisers' material is not edited by Forbes and appears online and in the magazine as "Forbes AdVoice."[5] (If it's for the print edition, Dvorkin reads it for tone, but says he does no more than that.) The print AdVoice column—limited to one per issue—appears in the table of contents and may run next to a related story. An online column is featured near relevant editorial content.

Giving advertisers direct access to an audience without previously approving the message is a big departure for media companies. The American Society of Magazine Editors' standards, revised in January 2011, are strict about separating ad content visually from editorial content, but they are silent on the access issue.[6]

Eric Hippeau, who has gone back to being a venture capitalist, calls this approach "turning your customers into publishers." Advertisers, he says, will not only create content that will increase traffic, but this will represent "a great diversification of revenues" away from advertising sold by the page view. Before Hippeau left the HuffPost, the company had just launched a program that charged flat fees and gave advertisers the opportunity to "have a conversation" with the site's audience through posts and responses. He believes that once companies start interacting with the audience in this environment, they will be hooked. "Once a brand starts that process, they are not going to stop. This is a great benefit to the media companies."[7]

Managing digital journalism properties often means stepping away from roles and job descriptions that were found in traditional operations. At AOL, executives have decided that content areas such as business or technology should become their own business units, or "towns" in the AOL patois.[8] And editors are increasingly responsible for determining the revenue potential of stories.

An explicit rendition of AOL's strategy can be found in a 57-page internal PowerPoint called "The AOL Way," which was leaked to Business Insider in February 2011. The handbook outlines AOL's plans to lower the cost of creating content while increasing revenue, with explicit targets; it was written a few weeks before AOL announced its deal to buy the Huffington Post.[9]

The company's rule of thumb is that the cost of acquiring a story should be no more than half the amount of ad revenue expected to come from that story.[10] An editor who wants to pay for a premium freelancer must also estimate the size of the audience for the assignment—in other words, the editor must cost-justify every story.[11] In the chart below, the company shows average costs and revenue by story type. The first column lists the department or source of the story, and the next column states the average cost of these stories. These figures are then matched with the "eCPM"—or effective cost (to advertisers) per thousand page views—and from that, AOL estimates the number of page views needed to break even on that story.[12]

Which AOL way for content?

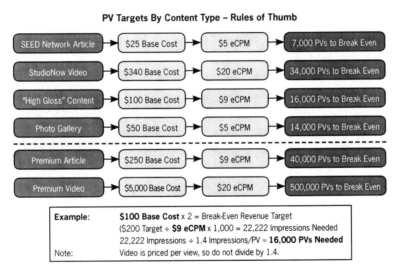

PV Targets By Content Type – Rules of Thumb

SEED Network Article	$25 Base Cost	$5 eCPM	7,000 PVs to Break Even
StudioNow Video	$340 Base Cost	$20 eCPM	34,000 PVs to Break Even
"High Gloss" Content	$100 Base Cost	$9 eCPM	16,000 PVs to Break Even
Photo Gallery	$50 Base Cost	$5 eCPM	14,000 PVs to Break Even
Premium Article	$250 Base Cost	$9 eCPM	40,000 PVs to Break Even
Premium Video	$5,000 Base Cost	$20 eCPM	500,000 PVs to Break Even

Example: **$100 Base Cost** x 2 = Break-Even Revenue Target
($200 Target ÷ **$9 eCPM** x 1,000 = 22,222 Impressions Needed
22,222 Impressions ÷ 1.4 Impressions/PV ≈ **16,000 PVs Needed**
Note: Video is priced per view, so do not divide by 1.4.

DEFINITIONS: PV = page views; eCPM = effective cost per thousand page views.
SOURCE: Reproduced from leaked AOL document, "The AOL Way," January 2011, page 17

One method of building traffic is to hop onto hot topics, the document advises. "Use editorial insight and judgment to determine production," the document says, offering as an example that if "Macaulay Culkin and Mila Kunis are trending because they broke up," someone should "write a story about Macaulay Culkin and Mila Kunis." And editors are told to always keep expenses in mind. The cost of content can run from $25 for a freelance article that needs 7,000 page views to break even, to a $5,000 video that will require a half-million streams to recover its costs.[13] Catchy headlines, such as "Lady Gaga Goes Pantless in Paris" (from AOL site StyleList.com) are important to entice readers from search.[14] Similarly, an article headlined "Benadryl for Dogs" should cost $15, because its revenue potential is around $26.[15] "We are heavily invested in analytics as this is the way to empower our editors and journalists," Neel Chopdekar, vice president at AOL Media, said in an interview shortly before "The AOL Way" was made public. He calls this "bionic journalism—the best of man and machine."

Paying freelancers by performance is not as unusual a practice as paying editorial staff that way. About.com, the general information website founded in 1995 and now owned by the New York Times, pays its expert writers, or "guides," by performance.[16] USA Today announced in early April that it is considering paying bonuses to writers based on page views.[17]

Digital companies, which lean heavily on part-time contributors or unpaid commenters, are constantly on the lookout for cheap labor. And mainstream news companies have long offered psychic, rather than financial, rewards to its reporters and editors.

Forbes' DVorkin is experimenting with pay schemes for blogging "contributors," whom Forbes compensates with a flat monthly fee. On top of that, Forbes pays a bonus if a writer reaches a certain target of unique visitors. (DVorkin declined to give details about pay at Forbes, but he did say that at True/Slant—the Web company he owned before coming to Forbes—contributors would typically earn about $200 per month, and some would get twice that much, counting their bonuses. A "few" earned several thousand dollars a month.) DVorkin said he'd like to add more metrics to the calculations—for example, Twitter followers or repeat visitors.

"In the newsroom, we are trying to develop different currencies to value success," says CNNMoney.com's Peacock. Journalists typically feel rewarded when their stories run on the front of a print publication, or lead the evening news. "We are trying to develop different kinds of 'front page' experiences for the journalists," Peacock says. But the new standards, such as the number of page views or comments, are often beyond an editor's control and are just as likely to be determined by readers, aggregators or bloggers.

Digital executives also must constantly decide when to deploy staff to work on new or experimental products that don't meet the new productivity tests. Tumblr, the social media microblogging platform, gets billions of monthly page views overall, but its value to most media companies is still negligible. Some journalists are fascinated with what it might become in terms of driving traffic or buzz—and their employers let them spend time with the platform, if only to be sure they don't miss out on something that might turn into the next Twitter. For example, GQ has a Tumblr site with just 12,000 followers—a tiny fraction of the print magazine's monthly circulation of 800,000. GQ's senior editor, Devin Gordon, says "Tumblr is a side project, but I care a lot about it." He and an editorial assistant limit themselves to no more than two hours per week posting Tumblr content.

Managers of digital operations must also deal with journalists who are able to establish a following on the basis of their own talents rather than the prestige or reach of the news organization. Andrew Sullivan's Daily Dish was responsible for 1 million monthly unique visitors, or about 20 percent of the traffic, at the Atlantic's site. But it was Sullivan's audience, not the Atlantic's; the blogger owned the brand equity. So when he moved to The Daily Beast in April 2011, he took his unique users with him. This phenomenon isn't entirely new, of course. Columnists like Walter Winchell would change employers in the glory days of the 1920s tabloid wars.[18] But in digital journalism, audiences can follow stars with great ease, and conceivably journalists with big individual followings could begin to keep, and try to make money from, data about their readers, rather than leaving that to their employers.

DVorkin says he is changing the way he judges the quality of a reporter. "It used to be a question of how they develop their sources. Now it's how they develop their sources *and* their audience." He expects Forbes journalists not just to cover news, but to be "maestros" of comments and of followers. And they have to be recruiters. "When we used to hire a reporter, we'd say, 'Show me some clips.' Now I say, 'Who is in your orbit? Who are your sources? Who do you know? Who can you convince to contribute?'"

The brutally competitive nature of digital journalism also extends to advertising sales, and many traditional media companies have a hard time justifying a large commitment to the effort simply because the returns, at least initially, can be so small. Consider the case of a company that publishes family-oriented magazines and a website. The company (which asked for confidentiality in return for providing its data) runs a profitable monthly print magazine, with free distribution of 400,000 copies within a top-five metro area. But its attempts to replicate its success on the Web haven't worked out. The site associated with the publication gets 200,000 unique users and 1.5 million page views per month. The expenses associated with the site amount to only around $181,000 per year, but that isn't quite covered by its ad revenue. Indeed, digital advertising accounts for just under 4 percent of the company's $4.68 million in annual ad revenue.[19] Of the company's 1,500 ad clients, 100 are online, and of those, only about 10 advertisers are exclusively digital

LIN Media sells an estimated $30 million in advertising from its Web and mobile efforts; that represents about 7 percent of total revenue, or a significantly larger percentage than many other local broadcasters claim.[20] But to put that figure into perspective, compare it to automobile advertising, which typically accounts for about 20 to 25 percent of total ad revenue for local broadcast companies.

These companies face an ongoing dilemma. If they didn't make an effort to sell digital advertising, they wouldn't lose much income—for now. But they believe that digital delivery of their content is bound to grow over time, so they are investing in working out pricing and customer relations even though the immediate return doesn't justify the effort. Whether they can play out these digital advertising calculations successfully depends on the quality of their management.

---

[1] "January 2011: Top U.S. Web Brands and News Sites" Nielsen, Feb. 11, 2011. http://bit.ly/evjGr6 and Compete.com, HuffingtonPost site analytics, April 22, 2011.

[2] Technorati.com, Huffington Post is the most influential blog of the 1.2 million tracked. April 22, 2011.

[3] Speech, Harvard Business School Club of New York Media Guru breakfast, April 5, 2011.

4 Lewis DVorkin, "9 big steps in 9 short months, now Forbes is building The New Newsroom," Forbes, March 1, 2011. http://bit.ly/fp1lwk

5 An example of this treatment is an article written by Eric Lai of SAP, "Video Killed the Radio Star, But Smartphones Did NOT Kill the Flip Cam," Forbes.com, April 14, 2011. http://bit.ly/glYrnr

6 "ASME Guidelines for Editors and Publishers," Magazine.org, Jan. 25, 2011. http://bit.ly/e3UZkS

7 Speech, Harvard Business School Club of New York Media Guru breakfast, April 5, 2011

8 Jessica Vascellaro, "Remaking AOL in Huffington's Image," Wall Street Journal, April 7, 2011. http://on.wsj.com/heuDE7

9 Nicholas Carlson, "Leaked: AOL's Master Plan," Business Insider, Feb. 1, 2011. http://read.bi/eTBJBJ

10 The AOL Way, January, 2011, page 28.

11 The AOL Way, January, 2011, page 17.

12 Ibid.

13 The AOL Way, January, 2011, slide 18.

14 Jennifer Barton, " Lady Gaga Goes Pantless in Paris," Stylelist, Dec. 10, 2010. http://aol.it/eTvVbJ

15 The AOL Way, January, 2011, slide 33

16 About.com guides get paid by the page view but do have a minimum guarantee. Dan Frommer, "About.com Cutting 10% Of Staff, Pay Cuts For Guides," Business Insider, Feb. 5, 2009. http://read.bi/i4NNV0

17 Jim Romenesko, "Report: Gannett to give page view bonuses to writers," Poynter, April 7, 2011. http://bit.ly/dE9p6f

18 Walter Winchell famously left the Evening Graphic and later joined the Daily Mirror in 1920s New York.

19 Details of the site's financial information:

Details of family-oriented magazine's website financials

	Estimated 2010
Total revenue print + digital	$ 4,684,000
Total revenue digital	$ 176,124
% digital	3.8%
Allocated cost of one in-house Web staffer	$ 42,000
Tech support	$ 48,000
Sales commissions	$ 35,225
Edit staff expense	$ 50,000
Site administration	$ 6,000
Estimated total expenses	$ 181,225
NET	$ (5,101)

SOURCE: Internal company documents.
The firm asked not to be identified in this report.

[20] When LIN reports its "digital revenue," it combines new-media sales with retransmission fees from cable companies in the sum. Based on discussions with Barry Lucas, a senior vice president at investment firm Gabelli & Co., who covers LIN, the authors estimate that half of the "digital revenue" represent new-media sales and half is retransmission fees.

Conclusion

"Here's the problem: Journalists just don't understand their business."

That's the diagnosis from Randall Rothenberg, a former New York Times media reporter who heads the Interactive Advertising Bureau, a trade group representing publishers and marketers.

Whether or not you agree with his sweeping characterization, it's clear that many sectors of the traditional news industry have been slow to embrace changes brought on by digital technology. They also have been flummoxed by competitors who invest minimally in producing original content but have siphoned off some of the most profitable parts of the business.

At the same time, digital journalism has created significant opportunities for news organizations to rethink the way they cover their communities. And in several organizations, old and new, we see promising signs that a transformed industry can emerge from the digital transition—one that is leaner, quicker and, yes, profitable.

We do not believe that legacy platforms should be disregarded or disbanded. It simply is not reasonable to assume that any company would cast aside the part of its business that generates 80 to 90 percent of its revenue. But we do think that companies ought to regard digital platforms and their audiences as being in a state of constant transformation, one that demands a faster and more consistent pace of innovation and investment.

To that end, we offer these recommendations:

- Digital platforms have been treated too often by traditional news organizations as just another opportunity to publish existing content. Many sites are filled with "shovelware"—content that amounts to little more than electronic editions of words and pictures from traditional platforms. But, as we have seen, publishers can build economic success by creating high-value, less-commoditized content designed for digital media. New York Magazine's successful site gets little traffic from print-edition stories; KSL.com's classfied ads are not part of its broadcast program; and the Dallas Morning News provides online football coverage that would be impossible to replicate in its sports section.

- Media companies should redefine the relationship between audience and advertising. They have spent a great deal of time and resources building masses of lightly engaged readers. And the industry has turned online ads into what Rothenberg calls low-value "direct-response advertising—a.k.a., junk mail." That kind of advertising is dependent on volume—a game publishers will never win when competing with behemoths like Facebook and Google. This is not a goal that can be accomplished just by the business side. Journalists must make a fuller commitment to understanding the audiences they have and the ones they want, and to revamping their digital offerings to ensure deeper loyalty.

- Media companies ought to rethink their relationships with advertisers. This doesn't mean allowing them to dictate coverage or news priorities. It does mean understanding that advertisers now have many more ways to reach customers than they used to and that some of these methods, such as social media, can be cheap and effective. News organizations have their own strengths: They produce journalism that is geared to their communities, and they employ sales forces who know their markets—both of which should give them a competitive advantage. They can act as guides to the digital era, helping companies produce new-media ads, place them online for maximum impact and learn such digital fundamentals as getting better positioning on search engines.

- News and marketing companies should develop alternatives to the impression-based pricing system (that is, pricing by CPM, or cost per thousand) that dominates online advertising. Small publishers have been successful selling ads by the week or month rather than by volume. Many large advertisers and ad agencies will insist on paying by the impression, but news organizations need to build upon their current pricing schemes by combining digital ads more effectively with broadcast or print, social-media outreach and other methods. Moreover, media companies must come up with ways to build content value into digital display ads; as others have also noted, too many of them are relics of a decade ago—boxes on a page that convey little of the information or appeal that historically made advertising valuable to consumers.

- News organizations must be vigilant about outright theft of their content, but they should also realize that most aggregators operate within the bounds of copyright law and are generating value for readers. This means news sites must do more than simply insert links (most of which are never clicked) within stories, and instead develop a thoughtful approach to understanding what topics best lend themselves to aggregation and how best to engage their readers in the effort.

- It is asking a lot to expect a legacy division—in news or ad sales—to embrace such a radically different world as digital. Retraining gets you only so far. Small, traditional news organizations may find it impossible to set up separate divisions. But bigger companies should analyze the potential in creating separate digital staffs, particularly on the business side. We did find successful companies with integrated digital and legacy departments, but others have demonstrated that they can compete more effectively by deploying committed digital-only teams that adapt to rapidly changing circumstances.

- Journalists must be prepared for continued pressure on editorial costs. There's an old rule of thumb in the newspaper world, that every 1,000 readers supports one newsroom staffer. That kind of thinking isn't going to hold in the digital world. We are likely to see a world of more, and smaller, news organizations, the most successful of which will leverage their staffs and audience by using aggregation, curation and partnerships with audiences to provide content of genuine value.

- Mobile digital devices represent a special challenge for news companies; for every successful new product or new platform, there will be others the company tried that didn't work. If a company can place small bets on many ventures, the probability increases that one will win.

- Any news site that adopts a pay scheme now should have very limited expectations for its success—at least on the Web. In the case of a print publication, requiring digital readers to pay may help to slow circulation losses, but that is hardly a long-term solution. A pay plan merged with an ambitious strategy to improve users' experience on mobile platforms has a much better chance to succeed.

We restate the bias we offered at the beginning of this report: We believe the public needs independent journalists who seek out facts, explain complex issues and present their work in compelling ways. We also believe that while philanthropic or government support can help, it is ultimately up to the commercial market to provide the economic basis for journalism. The industry has realized many of the losses from the digital era. It is time to start reaping some of the benefits.

Executive Summary

Chapter 1
News From Everywhere: *The Economics of Digital Journalism*

Large-scale competitive and economic forces are confronting news organizations, old and new. This chapter identifies 16 features of the digital world that are transforming the business of news, including changes in audience, aggregation, distribution, customer experience, cost structure, innovation cycles and advertising.

Chapter 2
The Trouble with Traffic: *Why Big Audiences Aren't Always Profitable*

Digital audiences often far outnumber those for broadcast or print news outlets, but online ad revenue is usually a fraction of what's earned in traditional news media. One reason is the difficulty sites have keeping readers' attention. The most loyal users typically make up a small part of the audience but look at the most pages per visit. Some news organizations are retooling their approach to derive more revenue from those users.

- Companies discussed: New York Times, Houston Chronicle, Los Angeles Times, Scout Analytics, Gawker Media, PBS, Dallas Morning News, Examiner.com, The Atlantic, Tumblr, New York Magazine, Newser, Mashable

Chapter 3
Local and Niche Sites: *The Advantages of Being Small*

Despite the general distress in the news industry, some community sites have succeeded. The economics of local and niche news providers are much different than those of large sites, and they capture some benefits by operating at such a small scale: low costs, local ties and creative online ad sales strategies. Networks such as Patch are attempting to be local to their audiences but national in their technology and ad sales, with uncertain success so far.

- Companies discussed: TBD, Main Street Connect, Patch, Baristanet, Alaska Dispatch, Batavian, Daily Candy

Chapter 4
The New New Media: *Mobile, Video and Other Emerging Platforms*

Journalism companies are grappling with a stream of innovations in digital media. Most organizations have tried to develop new ways to report and distribute stories, and many are making substantial investments to enable their work to appear on attractive new devices. Companies must constantly evaluate where to invest and how much. Video has been a special challenge. Publishers know that advertisers will pay a premium for video, but the video audience remains small at many news sites.

- Companies discussed: Wall Street Journal, The Daily, Wired, Sports Illustrated, Miami Herald, Dallas Morning News, CNN, New York Magazine, LIN Media, Forbes, Detroit Free Press

Chapter 5
Paywalls: *Information at a Price*

Publishers cite several reasons to charge for news online. One is to increase subscription revenue, another is to slow erosion in print audiences. Even before the Internet, subscription revenue didn't amount to much; Americans are used to paying little for their news. With few exceptions, digital pay plans have not been able to make up for declining advertising revenue offline. Digital subscriptions may pay off in the years to come, but only if media companies can persuade consumers to use, and pay for, mobile platforms like smartphones and tablets.

- Companies discussed: Wall Street Journal, Arkansas Democrat-Gazette, Dallas Morning News, Miami Herald, Financial Times, Newport Daily News, New York Times

Chapter 6
Aggregation: *'Shameless' – and Essential*

The arguments about companies like Huffington Post mask the reality that aggregation has long been a feature of the journalism business, and one that almost every news provider engages in today in some fashion. It makes economic sense to create and enrich content by linking to material that appears elsewhere, and aggregation is among the cheapest and most efficient ways to get users.

- Companies discussed: Huffington Post, AOL, Google, Yahoo, New York Magazine, Newser

Chapter 7
Dollars and Dimes: *The New Costs of Doing Business*

The notion of "trading dollars for dimes" captures the impact of digital distribution on the economics of the news business. Without having to make the steep investment that used to be required to launch a media business, low-cost local or topical sites have found it easier to build audiences. Legacy news producers face a trickier challenge: to cut costs and boost online revenue while trying to protect traditional advertising sources.

- Companies discussed: CT Mirror, Journal-Register, Breaking Media, Business Insider, The Atlantic, Detroit Free Press, Detroit News

Chapter 8
New Users, New Revenue: *Alternative Ways to Make Money*

Media companies that successfully make the transition to the digital world are developing new businesses and twists on old ones. These include selling marketing services to advertisers, beating Craigslist at its own game and broadening their sales beyond their own sites.

- Companies discussed: Houston Chronicle, KSL.com/Deseret News, McClatchy, Izea, Groupon, The Atlantic, Facebook

Chapter 9
Managing Digital: *Audience, Data and Dollars*

Every digital news organization faces relentless competition; some do better than others through high-quality management. Because digital news products are in a state of flux, it is critical for news companies to understand data and respond quickly. Hiring and compensation of journalists have been made more complicated as metrics have entered the picture. Some media companies are developing programs to encourage advertisers and marketers to contribute content directly in ways that wouldn't have been countenanced in the past.

- Companies discussed: Huffington Post, AOL, CNNMoney, LIN Media, Forbes, Tumblr, GQ

Acknowledgements

We owe a great debt to many people who contributed to this report. While we can't name them all here, we wish to thank some of those most deeply involved.

Nicholas Lemann, dean of Columbia's Journalism School, hatched the idea for the report and has consistently guided our efforts with wisdom and skill. Jeffrey Frank and Marcia Kramer carefully edited our copy and saved us from verbosity—or worse. Janice Olson took germs of our ideas and turned them into wonderful graphics. Emily Bell, director of the Tow Center for Digital Journalism, and Elizabeth Fishman, who oversees communications for the Journalism School, provided expert advice throughout.

Our families, friends and colleagues tolerated our absences with patience and provided wonderful insight that helped shape our findings.

Most importantly, we would like to thank the dozens of publishers, journalists and salespeople who opened their doors and books to us and dealt with our many questions. For all the difficulties that journalism faces these days, we were deeply impressed and encouraged by their commitment to this business, and to ensuring that citizens will continue to get the information they need to lead their lives.

The Authors

Bill Grueskin is dean of academic affairs and professor of professional practice at Columbia University's Graduate School of Journalism. He began his career at the Daily American in Italy, and then founded a weekly paper on the Standing Rock Sioux Indian Reservation in North Dakota. He later served as a reporter and editor at newspapers in Baltimore, Tampa and Miami. As the Miami Herald's city editor, he led local coverage of Hurricane Andrew; the Herald's overall coverage of the storm won the 1993 Pulitzer Prize for public service. Grueskin then worked for 13 years at the Wall Street Journal, including roles as deputy page-one editor, managing editor of WSJ.com and deputy managing editor/news. He joined Columbia's faculty in 2008. Grueskin has a bachelor's degree in classics from Stanford University and a master's degree in international economics and U.S. foreign policy from Johns Hopkins University's School of Advanced International Studies.

Ava Seave is a principal of Quantum Media, a New York City-based consulting firm focused on marketing and strategic planning for media, information and entertainment companies. Before co-founding Quantum Media in 1998, Seave was a general manager at three media companies: Scholastic Inc., the Village Voice and TVSM. She started her career as a photo editor for two horticulture magazines. Seave has adjunct appointments at the business and journalism schools at Columbia University. She is the co-author (with Jonathan Knee and Bruce Greenwald) of "The Curse of the Mogul: What's Wrong with the World's Leading Media Companies." Seave graduated from Brown University with a bachelor's degree in semiotics. She also holds a master's degree in business administration from Harvard Business School.

Lucas Graves is a PhD candidate in communications at Columbia University. His dissertation focuses on the fact-checking movement in American journalism as a window onto changes in the networked news ecosystem. Graves has worked as a technology and media analyst with various research firms and is a longtime magazine journalist, now on the masthead of Wired magazine. He co-authored the first report from the Tow Center for Digital Journalism, on the confusion over online media metrics. Graves holds a bachelor's degree in political science from the University of Chicago and master's degrees in communications and journalism from Columbia.

Disclosures

Grueskin served briefly as a consultant to the Providence Journal in early 2010. The Journal is owned by A.H. Belo Corp., which also owns the Dallas Morning News.

Seave served briefly as a consultant for New York Magazine in 2005 and for Conde Nast in consumer-marketing projects at various times in the past 10 years.